Mastering Go Network Automation

Network

Automation

Automating Networks, Container Orchestration,
Kubernetes with Puppet, Vegeta and Apache JMeter

Ian Taylor

Published by: GitforGits
Publisher: Sonal Dhandre
www.gitforgits.com
support@gitforgits.com

Printed in India

First Printing: March 2023

ISBN: 978-8196228545

Cover Design by: Kitten Publishing

Content

Preface

"Mastering Go Network Automation" is a structured beginning for network administrators looking to improve network efficiency, scalability, and security. This book provides a one-stop solution for all of your network administration needs, with comprehensive coverage of automation, security, containerization, monitoring, and performance testing.

Beginning with the fundamentals of creating a network automation lab with the EVE-NG network simulator and the Go programming language, readers will learn the step-by-step process of installing EVE-NG, followed by the importance of service mesh in automation and how it can simplify network operations.

The book delves deeply into critical topics such as deploying ingress controllers and implementing service mesh with Linkerd. Readers will learn about container-native storage, container storage management with Docker, and automating SSL certificates, firewall configuration, and network policies.

Monitoring and performance tuning are also covered in the book, including how to monitor container performance and automatically roll out updates. The book concludes with a discussion of performance testing strategies like load testing, stress testing, and scalability testing. It shows readers how to find performance bottlenecks and optimise their network with the help of tools like Vegeta and Apache JMeter through the use of real-world examples.

In this book you will learn how to:

- Setting up an EVE-NG network simulator, VIM IDE, kubeadm, and a comprehensive network automation lab to improve network efficiency, scalability, and security.
- Configuring ports, hosts, and servers using Go scripting to streamline network automation.
- Writing, testing, and validating network automation scripts to ensure smooth and reliable network administration.
- Building Docker images, running containers, and managing container deployments for efficient containerization.
- Automating load balancing, firewall configuration, and Kubernetes network policies for seamless network management.

- Working with popular tools such as Puppet, Zookeeper, Traefik, Envoy, and various Go networking packages.
- Automating SSL setup, container storage, container performance monitoring, and rolling updates.
- Using powerful load testing tools like Vegeta and Apache JMeter for efficient load testing, stress testing, and scalability testing to identify and eliminate performance bottlenecks.

GitforGits

Prerequisites

If you're a network administrator who wants to level up your game, "Mastering Go Network Administration" is the book for you. This book will help you become a more efficient, effective, and confident network administrator by providing clear explanations, practical examples, and comprehensive coverage.

Codes Usage

Are you in need of some helpful code examples to assist you in your programming and documentation? Look no further! Our book offers a wealth of supplemental material, including code examples and exercises.

Not only is this book here to aid you in getting your job done, but you have our permission to use the example code in your programs and documentation. However, please note that if you are reproducing a significant portion of the code, we do require you to contact us for permission.

But don't worry, using several chunks of code from this book in your program or answering a question by citing our book and quoting example code does not require permission. But if you do choose to give credit, an attribution typically includes the title, author, publisher, and ISBN. For example, "Mastering Go Network Automation by Ian Taylor".

If you are unsure whether your intended use of the code examples falls under fair use or the permissions outlined above, please do not hesitate to reach out to us at support@gitforgits.com.

We are happy to assist and clarify any concerns.

Acknowledgement

I owe a tremendous debt of gratitude to GitforGits, for their unflagging enthusiasm and wise counsel throughout the entire process of writing this book. Their knowledge and careful editing helped make sure the piece was useful for people of all reading levels and comprehension skills. In addition, I'd like to thank everyone involved in the publishing process for their efforts in making this book a reality. Their efforts, from copyediting to advertising, made the project what it is today.

Finally, I'd like to express my gratitude to everyone who has shown me unconditional love and encouragement throughout my life. Their support was crucial to the completion of this book. I appreciate your help with this endeavour and your continued interest in my career.

CHAPTER 1: GO ESSENTIALS FOR NETWORKS

Why Go for Networking?

Overview

Go, also known as Golang, is a programming language that was developed by Google in 2007. It is an open-source language that was designed with the goal of simplifying the process of developing high-performance network applications. The language's syntax is simple and easy to learn, and it is known for its efficiency, scalability, and reliability. Due to these features, Go has become increasingly popular for network programming and network automation.

Network programming refers to the development of applications that communicate over a network. These applications can include web servers, microservices, and other network-based services.

Features of Networking

Go provides a number of features that make it well-suited for network programming. These features include:

- Concurrency: Go has built-in support for concurrency, which allows developers to write applications that can handle multiple tasks simultaneously. This is particularly useful for network programming, where applications need to handle multiple requests and responses at the same time.
- Garbage collection: Go has an efficient garbage collector that automatically frees up memory that is no longer in use. This feature makes it easy for developers to write network applications without worrying about memory management.
- Standard library: Go comes with a comprehensive standard library that includes packages for handling networking, encryption, and other common tasks. This makes it easy for developers to write network applications without having to rely on third-party libraries.
- Error handling: Go has a robust error handling mechanism that makes it easy for developers to write applications that can handle errors gracefully. This is particularly important for network applications, which may encounter errors due to network connectivity issues.

In addition to these features, Go also has a number of tools and frameworks that make it easy to write network applications. These include:

The net package: The net package in Go provides a set of tools for handling networking tasks such as creating TCP and UDP sockets, and performing DNS lookups.

Goroutines: Goroutines are lightweight threads that make it easy to write concurrent applications in Go. They allow developers to handle multiple tasks at the same time without the need for complex threading code.

Channels: Channels in Go provide a mechanism for communicating between goroutines. They make it easy to write applications that coordinate multiple tasks.

Third-party libraries: Go has a vibrant ecosystem of third-party libraries that make it easy to write network applications. Some popular libraries include the Gorilla web toolkit, the Gin web framework, and the Colly web scraping library.

Overview of Network Automation

Network automation refers to the process of automating network-related tasks such as configuration, monitoring, and management. Go is well-suited for network automation due to its simplicity, efficiency, and scalability. Some of the features that make Go a good choice for network automation include:

- Simplicity: Go has a simple syntax that makes it easy to write and read code. This makes it easy for network administrators to write automation scripts without having to learn a complex programming language.
- Efficiency: Go is known for its efficiency, which makes it well-suited for tasks that require high performance. This is particularly important for network automation tasks, which may involve processing large amounts of data.
- Scalability: Go's built-in support for concurrency makes it easy to write automation scripts that can handle multiple tasks simultaneously. This is particularly useful for network automation tasks, which may involve managing multiple devices at the same time.
- Cross-platform support: Go can be compiled for multiple platforms, which makes it easy to write automation scripts that can run on different operating systems.

Go is a powerful programming language that is well-suited for network programming and network automation. Its simplicity, efficiency, and scalability make it a popular choice among developers and network administrators. With its built-in support for concurrency, efficient garbage collector, and comprehensive standard library, Go provides everything that developers need

Understanding Data Types

Go is a statically-typed programming language that provides a rich set of data types for representing different kinds of values. In this section, we will go through each of the data types available in Go and provide examples and illustrations for each of them.

Boolean

The Boolean data type is used to represent true or false values. In Go, the Boolean type is represented by the keyword bool. The two possible values for a Boolean variable are true and false. Below is an example:

var isSunny bool = true

In the above sample code, we declare a Boolean variable called isSunny and initialize it with the value true. This variable could be used to represent whether or not it is sunny outside.

Numeric Types

Go provides several different numeric types, including integers, floating-point numbers, and complex numbers.

Integer types

Integer types represent whole numbers, either positive or negative. Go provides several different integer types, which differ in the number of bits they use to represent the value. Some of the integer types available in Go are:

- int8: 8-bit signed integer
- int16: 16-bit signed integer
- int32: 32-bit signed integer
- int64: 64-bit signed integer
- uint8: 8-bit unsigned integer
- uint16: 16-bit unsigned integer
- uint32: 32-bit unsigned integer
- uint64: 64-bit unsigned integer

Below is an example:

var age int32 = 42

In the above sample code, we declare an integer variable called age and initialize it with the value 42. We use the int32 type to represent this value.

Floating-point types

Floating-point types represent decimal numbers, either positive or negative. Go provides two floating-point types: float32 and float64. The float32 type uses 32 bits to represent the value, while the float64 type uses 64 bits. Below is an example:

```go
var price float64 = 3.99
```

In the above sample code, we declare a floating-point variable called price and initialize it with the value 3.99. We use the float64 type to represent this value.

Complex types

Complex types represent complex numbers, which have a real part and an imaginary part. Go provides two complex types: complex64 and complex128. The complex64 type uses two 32-bit floating-point numbers to represent the real and imaginary parts, while the complex128 type uses two 64-bit floating-point numbers. Below is an example:

```go
var z complex128 = complex(1, 2)
```

In the above sample code, we declare a complex variable called z and initialize it with the value 1+2i. We use the complex128 type to represent this value.

String

The string data type is used to represent text. In Go, strings are represented as a sequence of characters enclosed in double quotes. Below is an example:

```go
var name string = "Alice"
```

In the above sample code, we declare a string variable called name and initialize it with the value "Alice". This variable could be used to represent a person's name.

Array

The array data type is used to represent a fixed-size collection of values of the same type. In Go, arrays are declared with a specific size and the elements are accessed by index. Below is an example:

```go
var numbers [5]int = [5]int{1, 2, 3, 4, 5}
```

In the above sample code, we declare an array called numbers with a size of 5 and initialize it with the values 1, 2, 3, 4, and 5. We use the [5]int type to represent this array.

Slice

The slice data type is used to represent a variable-size collection of values of the same type. In Go, slices are similar to arrays, but they do not have a fixed size and can be resized dynamically. Slices are declared using the same syntax as arrays, but without specifying a size. Below is an example:

```
var fruits []string = []string{"apple", "banana", "cherry"}
```

In the above sample code, we declare a slice called fruits and initialize it with the values "apple", "banana", and "cherry". We use the []string type to represent this slice.

Map

The map data type is used to represent an unordered collection of key-value pairs. In Go, maps are declared using the map keyword and the types of the keys and values. Below is an example:

```
var ages map[string]int = map[string]int{"Alice": 42, "Bob": 37}
```

In the above sample code, we declare a map called ages with string keys and integer values, and initialize it with the key-value pairs "Alice": 42 and "Bob": 37.

Struct

The struct data type is used to represent a collection of fields of different types. In Go, structs are declared using the type and struct keywords. Below is an example:

```
type Person struct {
    name string
    age int
}
var alice Person = Person{name: "Alice", age: 42}
```

In the above sample code, we declare a struct called Person with two fields: name of type string and age of type int. We then declare a variable called alice of type Person and initialize it with the values "Alice" and 42.

Interface

The interface data type is used to define a set of method signatures that a type must implement. In Go, interfaces are declared using the interface keyword. Below is an example:

```
type Shape interface {
    area() float64
    perimeter() float64
```

```go
}

type Circle struct {
    radius float64
}

func (c Circle) area() float64 {
    return math.Pi * c.radius * c.radius
}

func (c Circle) perimeter() float64 {
    return 2 * math.Pi * c.radius
}

var c Shape = Circle{radius: 1.0}
```

In the above sample program, we declare an interface called Shape with two methods: area() and perimeter(). We then declare a struct called Circle with a radius field of type float64 and implement the area() and perimeter() methods for the Circle type. Finally, we declare a variable called c of type Shape and initialize it with a Circle value.

The above explained are the main data types available in Go. By understanding how each of these data types works, you can write more effective and efficient Go code.

All about Loops!

In Go, there are three types of loops: the for loop, the while loop, and the range loop. Each of these loops is used to iterate over a sequence of values or a collection of data.

For Loop

The for loop is the most commonly used loop in Go. It is used to iterate over a sequence of values a specific number of times. The syntax of the for loop in Go is as follows:

```go
for initialization; condition; increment {
    // code to be executed
}
```

The initialization statement is executed once before the loop begins. The condition statement is evaluated at the beginning of each iteration, and if it is true, the code inside the loop is executed. The increment statement is executed at the end of each iteration.

Below is an example of using a for loop in Go to print the numbers from 1 to 10:

```go
for i := 1; i <= 10; i++ {
    fmt.Println(i)
}
```

In the above sample code, we use the := operator to declare and initialize the loop variable i to the value 1. The loop will continue as long as i is less than or equal to 10, and we use the i++ statement to increment i by 1 at the end of each iteration.

While Loop

In Go, there is no dedicated while loop like in other programming languages. However, you can simulate a while loop using a for loop with a single condition. Below is an example of using a while loop in Go to print the numbers from 1 to 10:

```go
i := 1
for i <= 10 {
    fmt.Println(i)
    i++
}
```

In the above sample code, we declare the loop variable i and initialize it to the value 1. We then use a for loop with a single condition i <= 10. The loop will continue as long as i is less than or equal to 10, and we use the i++ statement to increment i by 1 at the end of each iteration.

Range Loop

The range loop is used to iterate over the elements of a collection such as an array, slice, or map. The syntax of the range loop in Go is as follows:

```go
for index, value := range collection {
    // code to be executed
}
```

The index variable holds the index of the current element, and the value variable holds the value of the current element. The collection variable is the collection over which we want to iterate.

Below is an example of using a range loop in Go to iterate over the elements of an array:

```
numbers := [5]int{1, 2, 3, 4, 5}
for index, value := range numbers {
    fmt.Println("Index:", index, "Value:", value)
}
```

In the above sample code, we declare an array called numbers with five elements and initialize it with the values 1, 2, 3, 4, and 5. We use a range loop to iterate over the elements of the array and print the index and value of each element.

One thing to note about the range loop is that if you only want to iterate over the values of a collection, you can omit the index variable. Below is an example:

```
fruits := []string{"apple", "banana", "cherry"}
for _, value := range fruits {
    fmt.Println(value)
}
``
```

Infinite Loop

An infinite loop is a loop that continues to execute indefinitely. In Go, you can create an infinite loop using a for loop without a condition. Below is an example of using an infinite loop in Go:

```
for {
    // code to be executed
}
```

In the above sample code, we use a for loop without a condition. The code inside the loop will continue to execute indefinitely until the program is terminated.

You can also use the break statement to exit an infinite loop. Below is an example:

```
for {
```

```
    // code to be executed
    if condition {
        break
    }
}
```

In the above sample code, we use a for loop without a condition. The code inside the loop will continue to execute indefinitely until the condition is true. When the condition is true, we use the break statement to exit the loop.

Nested Loop

A nested loop is a loop inside another loop. In Go, you can use nested loops to iterate over multi-dimensional arrays or perform more complex iterations. Below is an example of using nested loops in Go to print a multiplication table:

```
for i := 1; i <= 10; i++ {
    for j := 1; j <= 10; j++ {
        fmt.Printf("%d x %d = %d\n", i, j, i*j)
    }
}
```

In the above sample code, we use two for loops. The outer loop iterates over the numbers from 1 to 10, and the inner loop iterates over the same numbers. Inside the inner loop, we print the multiplication table for the current numbers.

Early Exit

Sometimes you may need to exit a loop before it has finished iterating over all its elements. In Go, you can use the break statement to exit a loop early. Below is an example:

```
numbers := []int{1, 2, 3, 4, 5}
for _, value := range numbers {
    if value == 3 {
        break
    }
    fmt.Println(value)
}
```

In the above sample program, we use a range loop to iterate over the elements of the numbers slice. Inside the loop, we check if the current value is equal to 3. If it is, we use the break statement to exit the loop early. If it is not, we print the value.

Continue Statement

The continue statement is used to skip the current iteration of a loop and move on to the next iteration. Below is an example:

```
numbers := []int{1, 2, 3, 4, 5}
for _, value := range numbers {
    if value == 3 {
        continue
    }
    fmt.Println(value)
}
```

In the above sample program, we use a range loop to iterate over the elements of the numbers slice. Inside the loop, we check if the current value is equal to 3. If it is, we use the continue statement to skip the current iteration and move on to the next iteration. If it is not, we print the value.

In Go, loops are used to iterate over a sequence of values or a collection of data. The for loop is the most commonly used loop in Go and is used to iterate over a sequence of values a specific number of times. The while loop can be simulated using a for loop with a single condition, and the range loop is used to iterate over the elements of a collection. You can also use an infinite loop, a nested loop, or early exit statements such as `

Exploring Functions

Functions are an essential part of any programming language, and Go is no exception. A function is a block of code that performs a specific task. In Go, you can define and use functions to organize your code and make it more modular.

Defining Functions

A function in Go is defined using the func keyword, followed by the function name, a set of parentheses, and a set of curly braces. Below is an example of defining a function in Go:

```
func greet(name string) {
```

```
    fmt.Printf("Hello, %s\n", name)
}
```

In the above sample program, we define a function called greet that takes a single parameter called name, which is of type string. Inside the function body, we use the fmt.Printf function to print a greeting message that includes the name parameter.

Calling Functions

Once you have defined a function in Go, you can call it from other parts of your code. Below is an example of calling the greet function we defined earlier:

```
greet("John")
```

In the above sample code, we call the greet function and pass it the value "John" as the name parameter. When the function is called, it will print the message Hello, John.

Return Values

Functions can also return a value to the caller. In Go, you specify the return type of a function using the func keyword, followed by the function name, the parameters, and the return type. Below is an example of defining a function that returns a value in Go:

```
func add(a, b int) int {
    return a + b
}
```

In the above sample code, we define a function called add that takes two parameters called a and b, which are both of type int. The function body contains a single statement that returns the sum of a and b.

To call this function, you can store its return value in a variable:

```
result := add(3, 4)
fmt.Println(result)
```

In the above sample code, we call the add function with the values 3 and 4. The return value of the function is stored in the result variable, and then we use the fmt.Println function to print the value of result, which is 7.

Multiple Return Values

Go also supports returning multiple values from a function. To do this, you simply separate the return types with commas. Below is an example of defining a function that returns multiple values in Go:

```go
func divide(a, b float64) (float64, error) {
    if b == 0 {
        return 0, errors.New("division by zero")
    }
    return a / b, nil
}
```

In the above sample program, we define a function called divide that takes two parameters called a and b, which are both of type float64. The function body contains an if statement that checks if the b parameter is equal to 0. If it is, the function returns a zero value and an error message created using the errors.New function. If b is not equal to 0, the function returns the result of dividing a by b and a nil error.

To call this function, you can store its return values in separate variables:

```go
result, err := divide(4, 2)
if err != nil {
    fmt.Println(err)
} else {
    fmt.Println(result)
}
```

In the above sample program, we call the divide function with the values 4 and 2. The return values of the function are stored in the result and err variables. We use the if statement to check if the err variable is not nil. If it is not nil, we print the error message. Otherwise, we print the value of the result variable.

Variadic Functions

Go also allows you to define variadic functions, which are functions that can take a variable number of arguments. To define a variadic function, you simply add an ellipsis (...) before the type of the last parameter in the function definition. Below is an example of defining a variadic function in Go:

```go
func sum(numbers ...int) int {
    total := 0
    for _, number := range numbers {
        total += number
    }
    return total
}
```

In the above sample program, we define a function called sum that takes a variable number of arguments, all of which are of type int. Inside the function body, we use a for loop to iterate over all the arguments and add them up to a total variable.

To call this function, you can pass any number of int values as arguments:

```go
result := sum(1, 2, 3, 4, 5)
fmt.Println(result)
```

In the above sample program, we call the sum function with five int values as arguments. The return value of the function is stored in the result variable, and then we use the fmt.Println function to print the value of result, which is 15.

Anonymous Functions

Go also allows you to define anonymous functions, which are functions without a name that can be assigned to a variable or passed as an argument to another function. Below is an example of defining an anonymous function in Go:

```go
func main() {
    add := func(a, b int) int {
        return a + b
    }
    result := add(3, 4)
    fmt.Println(result)
}
```

In the above sample program, we define an anonymous function that takes two parameters called a and b, which are both of type int. We assign this function to a variable called add. Inside the main function, we call the add function with the values 3 and 4. The return value of the function is stored in the result variable, and then we use the fmt.Println function to print the value of result, which is 7.

To summarize, functions are an important aspect of Go programming. They allow you to organize your code, make it more modular, and reduce code duplication. With the various types of functions discussed above, you can write more efficient and scalable Go applications.

File Handling in Go

File handling is an important aspect of any programming language as it allows the programmer to read and write data to and from files. In Go, file handling is done through the os and io/ioutil packages. In this tutorial, we will cover some basic file handling operations in Go.

Creating a File

To create a new file in Go, you can use the os.Create function. This function takes the file name as a parameter and returns a pointer to the newly created file. Below is an example of creating a new file in Go:

```go
package main

import (
    "fmt"
    "os"
)

func main() {
    file, err := os.Create("example.txt")
    if err != nil {
        fmt.Println(err)
        return
    }
    defer file.Close()
    fmt.Println("File created successfully")
}
```

In the above sample program, we import the os and fmt packages. We then use the os.Create function to create a new file called example.txt. If the file is created successfully, we print a success message to the console. If there is an error while creating the file, we print the error message to the console.

Opening a File

To open an existing file in Go, you can use the os.Open function. This function takes the file name as a parameter and returns a pointer to the file. Below is an example of opening a file in Go:

```go
package main

import (
    "fmt"
    "os"
)

func main() {
    file, err := os.Open("example.txt")
    if err != nil {
        fmt.Println(err)
        return
    }
    defer file.Close()
    fmt.Println("File opened successfully")
}
```

In the above sample program, we use the os.Open function to open an existing file called example.txt. If the file is opened successfully, we print a success message to the console. If there is an error while opening the file, we print the error message to the console.

Writing to a File

To write data to a file in Go, you can use the io.WriteString function. This function takes two parameters: the file pointer and the data to be written to the file. Below is an example of writing data to a file in Go:

```go
package main

import (
```

```go
	"fmt"
	"io"
	"os"
)

func main() {
	file, err := os.Create("example.txt")
	if err != nil {
		fmt.Println(err)
		return
	}
	defer file.Close()

	data := "This is a sample text"
	_, err = io.WriteString(file, data)
	if err != nil {
		fmt.Println(err)
		return
	}
	fmt.Println("Data written successfully")
}
```

In the above sample program, we use the os.Create function to create a new file called example.txt. We then write the data "This is a sample text" to the file using the io.WriteString function. If the data is written successfully, we print a success message to the console. If there is an error while writing the data to the file, we print the error message to the console.

Reading from a File

To read data from a file in Go, you can use the io/ioutil.ReadFile function. This function takes the file name as a parameter and returns the contents of the file as a byte array. Below is an example of reading data from a file in Go:

package main

import (
	"fmt"

```
    "io/ioutil"
)

func main() {
    data, err := ioutil.ReadFile("example.txt")
    if err != nil {
        fmt.Println(err)
        return
    }
    fmt.Println
}
```

In the above sample program, we use the ioutil.ReadFile function to read the contents of the file called example.txt. If the file is read successfully, we print the contents of the file to the console. If there is an error while reading the file, we print the error message to the console.

Appending to a File

To append data to a file in Go, you can use the os.OpenFile function with the os.O_APPEND|os.O_CREATE|os.O_WRONLY flags. This function takes the file name as a parameter and returns a pointer to the file. Below is an example of appending data to a file in Go:

```
package main

import (
    "fmt"
    "os"
)

func main() {
    file, err := os.OpenFile("example.txt",
os.O_APPEND|os.O_CREATE|os.O_WRONLY, 0644)
    if err != nil {
        fmt.Println(err)
        return
    }
```

```go
    defer file.Close()

    data := "\nThis is some additional text"
    _, err = fmt.Fprintln(file, data)
    if err != nil {
        fmt.Println(err)
        return
    }
    fmt.Println("Data appended successfully")
}
```

In the above sample program, we use the os.OpenFile function to open the file called example.txt in append mode. We then append the data "This is some additional text" to the file using the fmt.Fprintln function. If the data is appended successfully, we print a success message to the console. If there is an error while appending the data to the file, we print the error message to the console.

Deleting a File

To delete a file in Go, you can use the os.Remove function. This function takes the file name as a parameter and deletes the file. Below is an example of deleting a file in Go:

```go
package main

import (
    "fmt"
    "os"
)

func main() {
    err := os.Remove("example.txt")
    if err != nil {
        fmt.Println(err)
        return
    }
    fmt.Println("File deleted successfully")
}
```

In the above sample program, we use the os.Remove function to delete the file called example.txt. If the file is deleted successfully, we print a success message to the console. If there is an error while deleting the file, we print the error message to the console.

Above we learned some basic file handling operations in Go. We learned how to create, open, write to, read from, append to, and delete a file. These file handling operations are essential for working with files in any programming language. Go provides an easy-to-use and efficient file handling mechanism, making it a great choice for any file-related operations.

Go Modules

Go introduced the concept of modules in version 1.11. Modules allow Go developers to manage dependencies more easily and improve the reproducibility of their builds. In this tutorial, we will learn about Go modules and how to use them in our projects.

What is a Module?

A module is a collection of related Go packages that are versioned together. A module has a unique name that identifies it, and it contains a go.mod file that specifies the module's dependencies and other metadata. A module can be used by other Go projects as a dependency.

Creating a Module

To create a new Go module, you can use the go mod init command followed by the name of the module. Below is an example:

```
$ go mod init example.com/hello
```

This command creates a new module called example.com/hello. It also creates a go.mod file that specifies the module's dependencies.

Adding Dependencies

To add a dependency to your Go module, you can use the go get command followed by the name of the package. Below is an example:

```
$ go get github.com/gorilla/mux
```

This command adds the github.com/gorilla/mux package as a dependency to your module.

It also updates the go.mod file to include the new dependency.

Managing Dependencies

Go modules provide several commands to manage dependencies. Here are some of the most commonly used commands:
- go mod init: Initializes a new module in the current directory.
- go mod tidy: Removes unused dependencies and updates the go.mod file to include the required dependencies.
- go mod vendor: Copies the module's dependencies to a vendor directory.
- go mod download: Downloads the module's dependencies.
- go mod verify: Verifies the module's dependencies and checks that their checksums match the expected values.

Below is an example of using the go mod tidy command:
```
$ go mod tidy
```

This command removes any unused dependencies and updates the go.mod file to include the required dependencies.

Using a Module

To use a module in your Go project, you can import the package using its full name. Below is an example:

```
package main

import (
    "example.com/hello/hello"
)

func main() {
    hello.Hello()
}
```

In the above sample program, we import the hello package from the example.com/hello module. We then call the Hello function from the hello package.

Publishing a Module

To publish a Go module, you need to make it available on a public repository. One option is to use the official Go module repository called pkg.go.dev. You can publish your module on this repository by following these steps:

- Create a GitHub repository for your module.
- Push your code to the GitHub repository.
- Tag a release for your module using the git tag command.
- Push the tag to the GitHub repository using the git push --tags command.
- Go to pkg.go.dev, and search for your module by its name.
- Click on the "Add version" button and select the tag you just created.

As we saw above, we learned about Go modules and how to use them in our projects. We learned how to create a new module, add dependencies, manage dependencies, use a module in our code, and publish a module on a public repository. Go modules provide an efficient and reproducible way of managing dependencies in Go projects. By using Go modules, we can ensure that our builds are consistent and reproducible, and that our dependencies are up-to-date.

My First Go Script

let us create a simple Go script that includes everything we've learned in this entire chapter. The given below is an example:

```
package main

import (
        "fmt"
        "os"
)

// Struct definition
type Person struct {
        Name    string
        Age     int
        Country string
}

// Function definition
```

```go
func (p Person) Greet() {
    fmt.Printf("Hello, my name is %s and I am %d years old. I am from %s.\n", p.Name, p.Age, p.Country)
}

func main() {
    // Variable declaration and initialization
    var num1 int = 5
    num2 := 10

    // Conditional statement
    if num1 < num2 {
        fmt.Println("num1 is less than num2")
    } else {
        fmt.Println("num1 is greater than or equal to num2")
    }

    // Loop
    for i := 0; i < 5; i++ {
        fmt.Println("Loop iteration:", i)
    }

    // Array
    numbers := [5]int{1, 2, 3, 4, 5}

    // Loop over array
    for _, number := range numbers {
        fmt.Println("Number:", number)
    }

    // Slice
    names := []string{"Alice", "Bob", "Charlie"}

    // Loop over slice
    for _, name := range names {
        fmt.Println("Name:", name)
    }
```

```go
// Struct instantiation
person := Person{Name: "John", Age: 30, Country: "USA"}

// Method call
person.Greet()

// File handling
file, err := os.Create("test.txt")
if err != nil {
        fmt.Println("Error creating file:", err)
        return
}
defer file.Close()

file.WriteString("Hello, world!")

fmt.Println("Script execution completed.")
}
```

This script includes a conditional statement, a loop, an array, a slice, a struct definition and instantiation, a method definition and call, and file handling. When executed, the script creates a file called test.txt and writes the string "Hello, world!" to it. The script also outputs various messages to the console to demonstrate the different features.

Summary

In this chapter, we covered the basics of the Go programming language. Go is a statically-typed language that was created at Google and is designed to be simple, efficient, and easy to use.

We started by discussing the installation process for Go, which involves downloading the Go distribution and setting up the environment variables on the computer. We also talked about the Go command-line interface, which is used to build, run, and test Go programs.

Next, we covered the basic syntax of Go, including variables, data types, operators, and control structures. We talked about how Go is a statically-typed language, which means that variables must be declared with their data type before they can be used. We also discussed the different data types available in Go, including integers, floating-point numbers, strings, and booleans.

We then moved on to more advanced topics, such as loops, functions, and file handling. Loops are used in Go to repeat a block of code a certain number of times, and we demonstrated how to use both the for and range loops in Go. Functions are used to encapsulate blocks of code that can be reused throughout a program, and we demonstrated how to define and call functions in Go. Finally, we talked about file handling in Go, which involves opening, reading, writing, and closing files using the built-in os package.

Throughout the chapter, we provided examples of Go code to demonstrate the different concepts. For example, we showed how to declare and initialize variables, how to use if/else statements to control program flow, and how to use arrays and slices to store collections of data. We also provided examples of how to use structs and methods to define custom types and operations on those types.

In addition to the technical details of Go, we also discussed some of the benefits and drawbacks of the language. We talked about how Go is designed to be efficient and scalable, making it well-suited for large-scale web applications and distributed systems. We also discussed how Go's simplicity and consistency can make it easy to learn and use. However, we also noted that Go may not be the best choice for every programming task, and that other languages may be better suited for certain types of applications.

Overall, this chapter provided a comprehensive introduction to Go, covering everything from the basics of the language to more advanced topics like functions and file handling. By the end of the chapter, readers should have a solid understanding of the fundamentals of Go and be able to write simple Go programs on their own.

CHAPTER 2: SETTING UP NETWORK AUTOMATION ENVIRONMENT

Components of a Network Automation Lab

A network automation lab is a testing environment that allows network engineers to simulate and test network configurations and automations before deploying them in a production environment. Go language is a popular language for network automation due to its simplicity, efficiency, and powerful libraries.

The following are the key components of a network automation lab with Go language:

Virtualization Environment

To create a network automation lab, the first step is to set up a virtualization environment that allows network engineers to simulate network devices such as routers, switches, and firewalls. There are several virtualization technologies available, including VirtualBox, VMware, and KVM. Once a virtualization environment is established, network engineers can create and manage virtual machines that represent network devices.

Network Devices

Virtual machines created in the virtualization environment represent network devices such as routers, switches, and firewalls. Network engineers can configure these devices using the device's command-line interface (CLI) or application programming interface (API) depending on the device. Configuration files for each device can be saved in a version control system like Git to track changes and revert to previous configurations if necessary.

Configuration Management

Configuration management is the process of automating network device configuration changes. Configuration management tools like Ansible, Chef, and Puppet allow network engineers to automate configuration changes across multiple network devices. Configuration management tools use templates and playbooks to define device configurations, which can be easily updated and deployed across the network.

Monitoring and Logging

Monitoring and logging are crucial components of network automation. Monitoring tools such as Nagios and Zabbix allow network engineers to monitor network device performance, availability, and uptime. Logging tools like syslog-ng and rsyslog enable network engineers to capture network events, errors, and warnings. Monitoring and logging tools provide valuable data that can be used to troubleshoot network issues and optimize network performance.

Testing Framework

Testing is an essential part of network automation. Testing frameworks like Ginkgo and Gomega allow network engineers to write and execute tests that verify network device configurations and automations. Testing frameworks can be used to ensure that network configurations are consistent across devices, that automation scripts are working correctly, and that network devices are operating as expected.

Scripting and Automation

Go language has powerful libraries for scripting and automation. The Go language standard library includes packages for HTTP, DNS, and TCP/UDP communications. The language's concurrency features allow network engineers to write efficient, concurrent network automation scripts that can manage multiple network devices simultaneously. Additionally, Go language has many third-party libraries that can be used for network automation, such as Netmiko and Nornir.

Security

Security is a critical aspect of network automation. Network automation scripts and tools must be secure to prevent unauthorized access to network devices and data. Network engineers can use secure coding practices and encryption to protect network automation scripts and data. Additionally, network automation scripts should be tested and audited regularly to ensure that they are working correctly and that they do not contain any security vulnerabilities.

To summarize, a network automation lab with Go language requires a virtualization environment, network devices, configuration management tools, monitoring and logging tools, testing frameworks, scripting and automation tools, and security measures. With these components in place, network engineers can develop, test, and deploy network configurations and automations with confidence.

Install EVE-NG Network Simulator

EVE-NG is a popular network simulator that allows network engineers to create and test complex network topologies without the need for physical hardware. In this guide, we will explain how to install EVE-NG network simulator on Linux.

Download EVE-NG Community Edition

The first step is to download the EVE-NG Community Edition from the official website. The download link can be found at https://www.eve-ng.net/index.php/download.

Choose the Linux version, and select the appropriate version based on your Linux distribution.

Install Dependencies

Before installing EVE-NG, we need to install some dependencies required for the application to run. These include Docker, QEMU, and libvirt.

To install Docker, run the following command in the terminal:

sudo apt-get install docker.io

To install QEMU, run the following command:

sudo apt-get install qemu-kvm libvirt-daemon-system libvirt-clients bridge-utils

After installation, enable the libvirtd service using the following command:

sudo systemctl enable libvirtd.service

Install EVE-NG

Once the dependencies are installed, navigate to the directory where you downloaded the EVE-NG Community Edition and extract the file.

tar xzvf eve-ng-x.x.x.tar.gz

Next, navigate to the extracted directory and run the following command to install EVE-NG:

sudo bash ./install-eve.sh

The installation process will take some time, and you will be prompted to enter your license key. If you do not have a license key, you can proceed with the community edition, which has some limitations.

Configure EVE-NG

Once the installation is complete, open a web browser and navigate to http://localhost:80. You should see the EVE-NG login page.

Enter the default username and password, which is admin and eve respectively. You will be prompted to change the password. After changing the password, you will be redirected to the EVE-NG dashboard.

Import EVE-NG Images

EVE-NG requires images to simulate network devices. These images need to be imported into the EVE-NG environment before they can be used.

To import an image, navigate to the Images section of the EVE-NG dashboard and click on the Import button.

Select the image file and click on the Import button. The image will be uploaded to the EVE-NG environment and added to the list of available images.

Create a Network Topology

Once the images are imported, you can create a network topology by dragging and dropping the devices onto the workspace.

To create a new topology, navigate to the Labs section of the EVE-NG dashboard and click on the Add Lab button. Give the topology a name and select the devices to be added.

Drag and drop the devices onto the workspace and connect them using the available interfaces.

Configure the Devices

After creating the network topology, you can configure the devices using the CLI or GUI interface. To access the CLI, right-click on the device and select Console.

To access the GUI interface, right-click on the device and select Web. This will open a web browser with the device's GUI interface.

Save and Export the Topology

After configuring the devices, save the topology by clicking on the Save button.
To export the topology, navigate to the Labs section of the EVE-NG dashboard and click on the Export button. Select the format in which you want to export the topology and click on the Export button.

Installing EVE-NG on Linux is a straightforward process that can be completed by following these steps. Once EVE-NG is installed, you can create and test complex network topologies without the need for physical hardware.

EVE-NG offers a range of features, including support for a wide variety of network devices, advanced routing protocols, and integration with external tools like Wireshark and GNS3.

By following this guide, you should be able to install EVE-NG on Linux and create and test network topologies. With EVE-NG, you can improve your network skills and become a more efficient network engineer.

Install Go for Network Automation Lab

Go is a popular programming language that is well-suited for network automation tasks. In this guide, we will walk through the process of installing Go on a Linux system.

Download Go

The first step is to download the latest version of Go from the official website. You can find the download link at https://golang.org/dl/. Choose the appropriate version for your system and download the binary file.

Install Go

Once you have downloaded the binary file, you need to extract it and install it on your system. Open a terminal window and navigate to the directory where you downloaded the binary file.

Use the following command to extract the file:

tar -C /usr/local -xzf go$VERSION.$OS-$ARCH.tar.gz

Replace $VERSION, $OS, and $ARCH with the appropriate values for your system. For example, if you downloaded go1.16.4.linux-amd64.tar.gz on a 64-bit Linux system, the command would be:
tar -C /usr/local -xzf go1.16.4.linux-amd64.tar.gz

Next, you need to add the Go binary directory to your system's PATH environment variable. Open the /etc/profile file in a text editor and add the following line at the end of the file:

export PATH=$PATH:/usr/local/go/bin

Save the file and close the text editor. To apply the changes, run the following command:

source /etc/profile

Verify Go Installation

To verify that Go has been installed correctly, open a terminal window and run the following command:

go version

This should display the version number of the installed Go binary. If you see an error message, check that you have correctly set the PATH environment variable.

Set up a Go Workspace

Before you can start writing Go code, you need to set up a Go workspace. A Go workspace is a directory hierarchy that contains Go source code, binaries, and libraries.

The workspace should have the following structure:

```
bin/
    hello              # command executable
pkg/
    linux_amd64/        # package object files
src/
    github.com/user/
        hello/
            hello.go     # command source
```

To create the workspace, first create a directory named go in your home directory:

mkdir ~/go

Next, create three subdirectories within the go directory:

```
mkdir ~/go/bin
mkdir ~/go/pkg
mkdir ~/go/src
```

Test the Go Installation

To test the Go installation, create a simple Go program. Open a text editor and create a file named hello.go with the following content:

package main

import "fmt"

func main() {
    fmt.Println("Hello, world!")
}

Save the file in the ~/go/src/hello directory. To build the program, open a terminal window and run the following command:

go install hello

This should create an executable file named hello in the ~/go/bin directory. To run the program, enter the following command:

~/go/bin/hello

This should display the message "Hello, world!" in the terminal window.

By following these steps, you should be able to install Go on your Linux system and set up a Go workspace. Go is a powerful language that can be used for network automation tasks, and by learning Go, you can improve your network automation skills and become a more efficient network engineer.

Install Vim IDE

Vim is a powerful text editor that is commonly used for network automation tasks. In this guide, we will walk through the process of installing Vim on a Linux system and setting it up for network automation.

Install Vim

The first step is to install Vim on your system. Most Linux distributions come with Vim pre-installed, but if it is not installed on your system, you can install it using the package manager.

For example, on Ubuntu, you can install Vim by running the following command:

sudo apt-get install vim

Install Vundle

Vundle is a plugin manager for Vim that makes it easy to install and manage plugins. To install Vundle, you need to download the Vundle plugin files and save them in the appropriate directory.

First, create the directory where you will store the Vundle files:

mkdir -p ~/.vim/bundle

Next, download the Vundle files using Git:

git clone https://github.com/VundleVim/Vundle.vim.git ~/.vim/bundle/Vundle.vim

Configure Vim

Once Vundle is installed, you need to configure Vim to use it. Open the .vimrc file in a text editor:

vim ~/.vimrc

Add the following lines to the file:

```
set nocompatible          " be iMproved, required
filetype off              " required

" set the runtime path to include Vundle and initialize
set rtp+=~/.vim/bundle/Vundle.vim
call vundle#begin()

" let Vundle manage Vundle, required
Plugin 'VundleVim/Vundle.vim'
```

```
" Add your plugins here (e.g. Plugin 'vim-airline/vim-airline')
Plugin 'vim-airline/vim-airline'
Plugin 'scrooloose/nerdtree'

call vundle#end()            " required
filetype plugin indent on    " required
```

This configures Vim to use Vundle and installs two plugins: vim-airline and NERDTree. You can add other plugins by following the same format.

Save the .vimrc file and exit the text editor.

Install Plugins

To install the plugins, open Vim and run the following command:

:PluginInstall

This will download and install the plugins listed in the .vimrc file.

Configure Plugins

Once the plugins are installed, you can configure them to suit your preferences. For example, to configure vim-airline, add the following lines to the .vimrc file:

```
" Configure vim-airline
let g:airline_theme='solarized'
let g:airline_powerline_fonts=1
```

This sets the theme to solarized and enables Powerline fonts.

To configure NERDTree, add the following lines to the .vimrc file:

```
" Configure NERDTree
map <C-n> :NERDTreeToggle<CR>
let NERDTreeIgnore=['\.pyc$', '\~$'] " ignore .pyc and backup files
let NERDTreeQuitOnOpen=1             " quit NERDTree when a file is opened
```

This sets up a keyboard shortcut to toggle the NERDTree window and configures some options.

By following these steps, you should be able to install Vim on your Linux system and set it up for network automation. Vim is a powerful text editor that can be customized with plugins to suit your needs, and by learning how to use it effectively, you can become a more efficient network engineer.

Configure Go Networking Libraries

After installing Go, you can start using its networking libraries to develop network automation applications. In this guide, we will walk through the process of configuring the Go networking libraries for network automation.

Import the Net Package

The Go net package provides a set of low-level networking primitives for TCP/IP, UDP, and Unix domain sockets. To use this package, you need to import it into your code:

```go
import (
    "net"
)
```

Create a TCP Listener

To create a TCP listener, use the net.Listen function:

```go
ln, err := net.Listen("tcp", ":8080")
if err != nil {
    // handle error
}
defer ln.Close()

for {
    conn, err := ln.Accept()
    if err != nil {
        // handle error
    }

    // handle connection
}
```

This code creates a TCP listener on port 8080 and waits for incoming connections. When a connection is received, it is passed to a separate goroutine for handling.

Create a UDP Connection

To create a UDP connection, use the net.Dial function:

```
conn, err := net.Dial("udp", "localhost:8080")
if err != nil {
    // handle error
}
defer conn.Close()

// send data
_, err = conn.Write([]byte("Hello, world!"))
if err != nil {
    // handle error
}
```

This code creates a UDP connection to localhost on port 8080 and sends a message.

Use the HTTP Package

The Go net/http package provides a set of functions for implementing HTTP servers and clients. To use this package, you need to import it into your code:

```
import (
    "net/http"
)
```

To create an HTTP server, use the http.ListenAndServe function:

```
http.HandleFunc("/", func(w http.ResponseWriter, r *http.Request) {
    fmt.Fprintf(w, "Hello, %q", html.EscapeString(r.URL.Path))
})

err := http.ListenAndServe(":8080", nil)
if err != nil {
    // handle error
}
```

This code creates an HTTP server that responds to requests with a greeting. The server listens on port 8080.

To make an HTTP request, use the http.Get function:

```
resp, err := http.Get("http://example.com/")
if err != nil {
    // handle error
}
defer resp.Body.Close()

body, err := ioutil.ReadAll(resp.Body)
if err != nil {
    // handle error
}
fmt.Println(string(body))
```

This code makes an HTTP GET request to example.com and prints the response body.

Use the SSH Package

The Go golang.org/x/crypto/ssh package provides a set of functions for implementing SSH servers and clients. To use this package, you need to import it into your code:

```
import (
    "golang.org/x/crypto/ssh"
)
```

To create an SSH client, use the ssh.Dial function:

```
config := &ssh.ClientConfig{
    User: "user",
    Auth: []ssh.AuthMethod{
        ssh.Password("password"),
    },
    HostKeyCallback: ssh.InsecureIgnoreHostKey(),
}
```

```go
conn, err := ssh.Dial("tcp", "localhost:22", config)
if err != nil {
    // handle error
}
defer conn.Close()

session, err := conn.NewSession()
if err != nil {
    // handle error
}
defer session.Close()

out, err := session.CombinedOutput("ls")
if err != nil {
    // handle error
}
fmt.Println(string(out))
```

This code creates an SSH client that connects to localhost on port 22 and executes the "ls" command.

Configure Ports with Go

In network automation, configuring ports is a common task. In this guide, we will explore how to use Go scripting and its libraries to configure ports.

Import "os/exec" Package

The "os/exec" package provides a way to execute external commands. To use this package, import it into your code:

```go
import (
    "os/exec"
)
```

Use "exec.Command" Function

To run a command, use the "exec.Command" function:

```
cmd := exec.Command("ifconfig", "eth0", "192.168.1.10/24")
err := cmd.Run()
if err != nil {
    // handle error
}
```

This code runs the "ifconfig" command to configure the IP address of "eth0" interface.

Use "exec.Output" Function

To capture the output of a command, use the "exec.Output" function:

```
cmd := exec.Command("ifconfig", "eth0")
output, err := cmd.Output()
if err != nil {
    // handle error
}
fmt.Println(string(output))
```

This code runs the "ifconfig" command to get the configuration of the "eth0" interface and prints the output to the console.

Use "os/exec" Package to Configure Ports

To configure multiple ports, you can use the "os/exec" package to execute multiple commands:

```
cmds := []string{
    "ifconfig eth0 192.168.1.10/24",
    "ifconfig eth1 10.0.0.1/24",
}

for _, cmdStr := range cmds {
    cmd := exec.Command("sh", "-c", cmdStr)
    err := cmd.Run()
    if err != nil {
        // handle error
    }
}
```

This code executes two commands to configure the IP addresses of the "eth0" and "eth1" interfaces.

Use "os" Package to Configure Ports

You can also use the "os" package to configure ports:

```
file,            err            :=            os.OpenFile("/etc/network/interfaces",
os.O_APPEND|os.O_WRONLY, 0644)
if err != nil {
    // handle error
}
defer file.Close()

_, err = file.WriteString("\nauto eth0\niface eth0 inet static\naddress
192.168.1.10\nnetmask 255.255.255.0\ngateway 192.168.1.1\n")
if err != nil {
    // handle error
}
```

This code opens the "/etc/network/interfaces" file and appends the configuration for the "eth0" interface.

In summary, Go scripting and its libraries provide a powerful and flexible way to configure ports in network automation. By using the "os/exec" and "os" packages, you can execute external commands and manipulate files to configure ports on network devices.

Summary

In this chapter, we focused on setting up a network automation lab using EVE-NG network simulator and Go language. The first step we took was to discuss the requirements for setting up the lab. This included the hardware requirements, software requirements, and network topology.

Next, we moved on to the installation process of EVE-NG on Linux. We discussed the prerequisites for installing EVE-NG, such as Ubuntu Linux, VirtualBox, and the EVE-NG ISO image. We then went through the step-by-step process of installing and configuring EVE-NG. This involved creating a new virtual machine, configuring the virtual machine settings, and booting up the virtual machine to install EVE-NG.

After installing EVE-NG, we discussed how to install and configure VIM IDE for network automation lab. VIM is a powerful text editor that is widely used by network automation engineers. We went through the process of installing VIM and configuring it for network automation purposes. This included installing the necessary plugins and setting up the configuration file.

Finally, we discussed the installation and configuration of Go networking libraries. This involved installing the necessary libraries and setting up the environment variables. We discussed the various Go libraries that are useful for network automation, such as net/http, net/smtp, and net/dns. We also went through some sample code that demonstrated how to use these libraries for network automation tasks.

In summary, this chapter provided a comprehensive guide on setting up a network automation lab using EVE-NG network simulator and Go language. We covered the prerequisites for setting up the lab, the step-by-step process of installing and configuring EVE-NG, the installation and configuration of VIM IDE, and the installation and configuration of Go networking libraries. With this knowledge, network automation engineers can create their own network automation labs and use them for testing and developing network automation scripts and applications.

CHAPTER 3:
CONFIGURING MODERN
NETWORKS

Components of Modern Networks

Hosts, servers, and networks are three essential components of modern computing and communication systems. Understanding their importance is crucial for professionals working in the fields of IT, networking, and system administration. In this response, we will explore the role of hosts, servers, and networks in detail and explain why they are critical to the functioning of modern computing systems.

Hosts

Hosts refer to individual devices or machines that are connected to a network. Examples of hosts include desktop computers, laptops, smartphones, and tablets. Hosts can communicate with each other over a network by exchanging data packets. The importance of hosts lies in their ability to connect to other devices and access shared resources such as printers, files, and databases. Hosts are also critical for accessing and using applications and services that are hosted on servers.

Servers

Servers are computer programs or machines that provide services or resources to other devices on a network. Examples of servers include web servers, email servers, file servers, and database servers. The importance of servers lies in their ability to provide shared resources and services to multiple hosts over a network. Servers enable businesses and organizations to share information and collaborate effectively by providing a centralized platform for data storage, communication, and collaboration.

In addition to sharing resources and services, servers also perform critical functions such as security, data backup and recovery, and load balancing. Security servers, for example, protect a network by detecting and blocking malicious traffic, while backup servers ensure that data is stored safely and can be recovered in case of a disaster. Load balancing servers distribute network traffic across multiple servers to ensure that the network can handle a large number of requests and remain available even during peak usage periods.

Networks

Networks are the backbone of modern computing systems. A network is a collection of devices that are connected together to exchange data and share resources. The importance of networks lies in their ability to connect hosts and servers to each other, enabling them to communicate and share resources. Networks are critical for businesses and organizations because they enable employees to collaborate effectively and share information, regardless of their location.

Types of Networks

There are several types of networks, including local area networks (LANs), wide area networks (WANs), and virtual private networks (VPNs). LANs are used to connect devices within a small geographic area, such as an office or building. WANs, on the other hand, are used to connect devices over a larger geographic area, such as a city or country. VPNs are used to connect devices over the internet securely.

The importance of networks lies not only in their ability to connect devices and enable communication but also in their ability to provide security and reliability. Network security is critical to protecting sensitive data and preventing unauthorized access to a network. Network reliability is essential to ensuring that a network remains available and functioning even during periods of high usage.

To summarize, hosts, servers, and networks are critical components of modern computing and communication systems. Hosts enable devices to connect to each other and share resources, servers provide services and resources to other devices on a network, and networks connect hosts and servers to each other, enabling them to communicate and share resources. Understanding the importance of hosts, servers, and networks is essential for professionals working in the fields of IT, networking, and system administration. By recognizing the critical role that these components play in modern computing, professionals can design and manage effective and efficient systems that meet the needs of businesses and organizations.

Configure Hosts

In network automation, configuring hosts is a common task. In this guide, we will explore how to use Go scripting and the installed libraries to configure hosts.

Import "os/exec" Package

The "os/exec" package provides a way to execute external commands. To use this package, import it into your code:

```
import (
    "os/exec"
)
```

Use "exec.Command" Function to Run Command

To run a command, use the "exec.Command" function:

```
cmd := exec.Command("hostnamectl", "set-hostname", "new-hostname")
err := cmd.Run()
if err != nil {
    // handle error
}
```

This code runs the "hostnamectl" command to change the hostname of the host to "new-hostname".

Use "exec.Output" Function to Capture Output

To capture the output of a command, use the "exec.Output" function:

```
cmd := exec.Command("uname", "-r")
output, err := cmd.Output()
if err != nil {
    // handle error
}
fmt.Println(string(output))
```

This code runs the "uname -r" command to get the kernel version of the host and prints the output to the console.

Use "os/exec" Package to Configure Multiple Hosts

To configure multiple hosts, you can use the "os/exec" package to execute multiple commands:

```
cmds := []string{
    "hostnamectl set-hostname new-hostname-1",
    "hostnamectl set-hostname new-hostname-2",
}

for _, cmdStr := range cmds {
    cmd := exec.Command("sh", "-c", cmdStr)
    err := cmd.Run()
    if err != nil {
        // handle error
    }
```

```
}
```

This code executes two commands to change the hostname of the two hosts.

Use "os" Package to Configure Hosts

You can also use the "os" package to configure hosts:

```
err := os.Setenv("http_proxy", "http://proxy.example.com:8080")
if err != nil {
    // handle error
}
```

This code sets the "http_proxy" environment variable to "http://proxy.example.com:8080" on the host.

In summary, Go scripting and the installed libraries provide a powerful and flexible way to configure hosts in network automation. By using the "os/exec" and "os" packages, you can execute external commands and manipulate environment variables to configure hosts on network devices.

Configure Servers

In network automation, configuring servers is a common task. In this guide, we will explore how to use Go scripting and the installed libraries to configure servers similar to host configuration. The process an the use of package is almost same as below:

Import "os/exec" Package

The "os/exec" package provides a way to execute external commands. To use this package, import it into your code:

```
import (
    "os/exec"
)
```

Use "exec.Command" Function to Run Command

To run a command, use the "exec.Command" function:

```go
cmd := exec.Command("systemctl", "start", "httpd.service")
err := cmd.Run()
if err != nil {
    // handle error
}
```

This code runs the "systemctl" command to start the "httpd" service on the server.

Use "exec.Output" Function to Capture Output

To capture the output of a command, use the "exec.Output" function:

```go
cmd := exec.Command("uname", "-r")
output, err := cmd.Output()
if err != nil {
    // handle error
}
fmt.Println(string(output))
```

This code runs the "uname -r" command to get the kernel version of the server and prints the output to the console.

Use "os/exec" Package to Configure Multiple Servers

To configure multiple servers, you can use the "os/exec" package to execute multiple commands:

```go
cmds := []string{
    "systemctl start httpd.service",
    "systemctl start nginx.service",
}

for _, cmdStr := range cmds {
    cmd := exec.Command("sh", "-c", cmdStr)
    err := cmd.Run()
    if err != nil {
        // handle error
    }
}
```

This code executes two commands to start the "httpd" and "nginx" services on the servers.

Use "os" Package to Configure Servers

You can also use the "os" package to configure servers:

```
err := os.Mkdir("/var/www/html/mywebsite", 0755)
if err != nil {
    // handle error
}
```

This code creates a directory named "mywebsite" under "/var/www/html" on the server.

In summary, Go scripting and the installed libraries provide a powerful and flexible way to configure servers in network automation. By using the "os/exec" and "os" packages, you can execute external commands and manipulate files and directories to configure servers on network devices.

Configure Network Encryption

Network encryption is a crucial aspect of network security. In this guide, we will explore how to use Go scripting and the installed libraries to configure network encryption.

Import "crypto/tls" Package

The "crypto/tls" package provides a way to create TLS (Transport Layer Security) connections. To use this package, import it into your code:

```
import (
    "crypto/tls"
)
```

Use "tls.Dial" Function to Create TLS Connection

To create a TLS connection, use the "tls.Dial" function:

```
conn, err := tls.Dial("tcp", "example.com:443", &tls.Config{})
if err != nil {
    // handle error
}
```

```
defer conn.Close()
```

This code creates a TLS connection to the "example.com" server on port 443.

Use "tls.Listen" Function to Listen TLS Connections

To listen for TLS connections, use the "tls.Listen" function:

```
cert, err := tls.LoadX509KeyPair("cert.pem", "key.pem")
if err != nil {
    // handle error
}

config := tls.Config{Certificates: []tls.Certificate{cert}}

ln, err := tls.Listen("tcp", ":443", &config)
if err != nil {
    // handle error
}
defer ln.Close()

for {
    conn, err := ln.Accept()
    if err != nil {
        // handle error
    }
    go handleConnection(conn)
}
```

This code listens for TLS connections on port 443 and calls the "handleConnection" function to handle each connection.

Use "tls.Config" Struct to Configure TLS Connection

The "tls.Config" struct provides many options to configure the TLS connection. For example, you can set the minimum TLS version, the cipher suites, and the client authentication policy:

```
config := tls.Config{
```

```
    MinVersion: tls.VersionTLS12,
    CipherSuites: []uint16{
       tls.TLS_RSA_WITH_AES_256_CBC_SHA,
       tls.TLS_RSA_WITH_AES_128_CBC_SHA,
    },
    ClientAuth: tls.RequireAndVerifyClientCert,
    ClientCAs:  certPool,
}
```

This code sets the minimum TLS version to 1.2, the cipher suites to AES-256 and AES-128, and requires client authentication.

Use "crypto/rand" Package to Generate Random Numbers

The "crypto/rand" package provides a way to generate random numbers. To use this package, import it into your code:

```
import (
    "crypto/rand"
)
```

Use "crypto/tls" Package to Create Self-Signed Certificate

To create a self-signed certificate for testing purposes, use the "crypto/tls" package:

```
template := x509.Certificate{
    SerialNumber: big.NewInt(1),
    Subject: pkix.Name{
       CommonName:  "example.com",
       Organization: []string{"Acme Inc."},
    },
    NotBefore:          time.Now(),
    NotAfter:           time.Now().AddDate(1, 0, 0),
    KeyUsage:                          x509.KeyUsageKeyEncipherment |
x509.KeyUsageDigitalSignature,
    ExtKeyUsage:         []x509.ExtKeyUsage{x509.ExtKeyUsageServerAuth},
    BasicConstraintsValid: true,
}
```

```go
key, err := rsa.GenerateKey(rand.Reader, 2048)
if err != nil {
   // handle error
}

derBytes, err := x509.CreateCertificate(rand.Reader, &template, &template,
&key.PublicKey, key)
if err != nil {
   // handle error
}

cert, err := tls.X509KeyPair(derBytes, key)
if err != nil {
// handle error
}

config := tls.Config{Certificates: []tls.Certificate{cert}}

ln, err := tls.Listen("tcp", ":443", &config)
if err != nil {
// handle error
}
defer ln.Close()

for {
conn, err := ln.Accept()
if err != nil {
// handle error
}
go handleConnection(conn)
}
```

This code creates a self-signed certificate with the CommonName "example.com" and listens for TLS connections on port 443.

Verify the TLS Connection

To verify the TLS connection, use the "tls.ConnectionState" struct:

```
conn, err := tls.Dial("tcp", "example.com:443", &tls.Config{})
if err != nil {
// handle error
}
defer conn.Close()

state := conn.ConnectionState()
if len(state.PeerCertificates) == 0 {
// handle error
}

cert := state.PeerCertificates[0]
fmt.Println(cert.Subject.CommonName)
```

This code prints the CommonName of the peer certificate.

With these tools, you can secure your network communication and ensure the privacy and integrity of your data.

Test Simulator, Ports, Hosts and Server

Testing a network automation lab is a crucial step to ensure that everything is properly configured and working as expected. In this section, we will discuss various testing methods that can be used to verify the functionality of the installed simulator, installed libraries, ports, hosts, and servers.

Testing the Simulator

To test the simulator, you can create a virtual network topology and verify that the network devices are communicating with each other as expected. For example, you can create a network topology with two routers and two hosts, and configure the routers to communicate with each other via OSPF.

Once the network topology is created, you can verify the connectivity between the hosts using the ping command. You can also verify the routing table on the routers to ensure that they have learned the routes via OSPF.

Testing Installed Libraries

To test the installed libraries, you can create a simple script that uses the library functions and verifies the output. For example, you can use the net package to create a TCP connection to a remote host and send some data.

```
package main

import (
    "fmt"
    "net"
)

func main() {
    conn, err := net.Dial("tcp", "google.com:80")
    if err != nil {
        fmt.Println("Error:", err)
        return
    }
    defer conn.Close()

    fmt.Fprintf(conn, "GET / HTTP/1.0\r\n\r\n")
    response := make([]byte, 1024)
    conn.Read(response)
    fmt.Println(string(response))
}
```

This script creates a TCP connection to Google's web server and sends a GET request to retrieve the homepage. The response is then printed to the console.

You can also test the cryptography libraries by encrypting and decrypting some data using the AES encryption algorithm. For example, you can use the crypto/aes package to encrypt and decrypt a string.

```
package main

import (
    "crypto/aes"
```

```go
    "crypto/cipher"
    "fmt"
)

func main() {
    key := []byte("my-secret-key-123") // 16-byte key
    plaintext := []byte("Hello, world!")

    block, err := aes.NewCipher(key)
    if err != nil {
        fmt.Println("Error:", err)
        return
    }

    ciphertext := make([]byte, aes.BlockSize+len(plaintext))
    iv := ciphertext[:aes.BlockSize]
    if _, err := cipher.NewCTR(block, iv).XORKeyStream(ciphertext[aes.BlockSize:], plaintext); err != nil {
        fmt.Println("Error:", err)
        return
    }

    fmt.Println("Ciphertext:", ciphertext)
    fmt.Println("Plaintext:", plaintext)
}
```

This script uses the AES encryption algorithm to encrypt the plaintext "Hello, world!" using a 16-byte key. The ciphertext and plaintext are then printed to the console.

Testing Ports

To test the ports, you can use the telnet command to connect to a remote host on a specific port. For example, you can connect to Google's web server on port 80 and send a GET request to retrieve the homepage.

```
$ telnet google.com 80
Trying 172.217.5.78...
Connected to google.com.
```

Escape character is '^]'.
GET / HTTP/1.0

HTTP/1.0 200 OK
Date: Fri, 26 Mar 2021 04:08:11 GMT
...

This command connects to Google's web server on port 80 and sends a GET request to retrieve the homepage. The response is then printed to the console.

You can also use the netstat command to view the open ports on a local system.

$ netstat -an |

This command displays a list of all open network connections and listening ports on the local system.

Testing Hosts

To test the hosts, you can use the ping command to verify the connectivity between two hosts on the network. For example, you can ping a remote host to verify that it is reachable and responding.

$ ping google.com
PING google.com (172.217.5.78) 56(84) bytes of data.
64 bytes from lga25s62-in-f14.1e100.net (172.217.5.78): icmp_seq=1 ttl=117 time=18.6 ms
64 bytes from lga25s62-in-f14.1e100.net (172.217.5.78): icmp_seq=2 ttl=117 time=17.6 ms

...

This command sends ICMP echo requests to Google's web server and prints the response to the console.

You can also use the nmap command to scan a remote host for open ports and services.

$ nmap google.com
Starting Nmap 7.80 (https://nmap.org) at 2021-03-26 01:13 PDT
Nmap scan report for google.com (172.217.5.78)
Host is up (0.014s latency).

This command performs a port scan on Google's web server and displays a list of open ports and services.

Testing Servers

To test the servers, you can use the curl command to send HTTP requests to a web server and verify the response. For example, you can retrieve the homepage of Google's web server using the curl command.

```
$ curl http://google.com
<!doctype html><html itemscope="" itemtype="http://schema.org/WebPage"
lang="en"><head><meta content="Search the world's information, including
webpages, images, videos and more. Google has many special features to help
you find exactly what you're looking for." name="description"><meta
content="noodp" name="robots"><meta content="text/html; charset=UTF-8"...
```

This command sends an HTTP GET request to Google's web server and prints the response to the console.

You can also use the openssl command to test the SSL/TLS encryption on a web server.
```
$ openssl s_client -connect google.com:443
CONNECTED(00000003)
...
```

This command connects to Google's web server on port 443 and initiates an SSL/TLS handshake. The SSL/TLS certificate information is then printed to the console.

Overall, we discussed various testing methods that can be used to verify the functionality of the installed simulator, installed libraries, ports, hosts, and servers. By using these testing methods, you can ensure that your network automation lab is properly configured and working as expected.

Summary

In this chapter, we discussed how to configure ports, hosts, and servers using Go scripting and the installed libraries. This involved creating Go scripts to configure network interfaces, IP addresses, and network services.

We also discussed how to configure network encryption using Go scripting and the installed libraries. This involved setting up SSL/TLS encryption on web servers and verifying the SSL/TLS certificate using the openssl command.

Finally, we discussed various testing methods that can be used to verify the functionality of the installed simulator, installed libraries, ports, hosts, and servers. These testing methods included using the netstat command to check for open network connections and listening ports, using the ping command to test connectivity between hosts, using the nmap command to scan a remote host for open ports and services, using the curl command to send HTTP requests to a web server and verify the response, and using the openssl command to test SSL/TLS encryption on a web server.

Overall, setting up a network automation lab requires a combination of software tools, programming languages, and networking knowledge. By following the step-by-step process outlined in this chapter, you can set up your own network automation lab and start automating your network infrastructure.

CHAPTER 4: WRITE, TEST AND VALIDATE AUTOMATION SCRIPTS

Understanding Go Network Automation Scripts

Network automation scripts using Go are programs that automate the management and configuration of network devices. These scripts are designed to help network engineers and administrators to simplify their work and reduce the time and effort required to manage complex networks.

In general, network automation scripts can be used for a variety of tasks, including device configuration, monitoring, and troubleshooting. For example, a script might be used to configure a router or switch with specific settings, such as IP addresses or routing protocols. Another script might be used to monitor network traffic or collect data on network performance.

Go is well-suited for network automation scripting due to its performance and concurrency features. Go is a compiled language that can execute code very quickly, making it ideal for processing large amounts of network data or making configuration changes to many devices at once. Go also has built-in support for concurrency, which allows multiple tasks to be executed simultaneously, making it easier to manage and monitor multiple devices at once.

Procedure to Code Network Automation Scripts

To create a network automation script using Go, the first step is to identify the tasks that need to be automated. This might involve gathering information about the devices on the network, such as their IP addresses, configuration settings, or status. Once this information has been collected, the script can be written to perform the desired tasks, such as configuring devices or monitoring network traffic.

One common approach to network automation scripting is to use a library or framework that provides pre-built functionality for common network tasks. For example, the "netconf" library provides a set of tools for managing network devices using the NETCONF protocol. Similarly, the "go-netbox" library provides a set of tools for interacting with the NetBox IPAM and DCIM system. These libraries can help to simplify the process of writing network automation scripts by providing a higher-level interface to the network devices.

Another important consideration when writing network automation scripts is error handling. Network devices can be unpredictable, and errors can occur for a variety of reasons, such as configuration conflicts or network outages. Therefore, it is important to design scripts that can handle errors gracefully and provide useful feedback to the user. This might involve logging error messages, sending notifications to the user, or automatically attempting to recover from errors.

Ways to Write Automation Scripts

One example of a network automation script using Go is a tool for configuring network devices with Ansible. Ansible is a popular open-source tool for automating IT infrastructure, including network devices. To use Ansible with network devices, a "module" must be created that provides the necessary functionality for interacting with the devices. A Go-based module can be created using the "go-ansible" library, which provides a set of tools for creating Ansible modules using Go.

Another example of a network automation script using Go is a tool for monitoring network traffic using the SNMP protocol. SNMP (Simple Network Management Protocol) is a standard protocol for monitoring and managing network devices. Using the "gosnmp" library, a Go-based tool can be created that queries network devices using SNMP and collects data on network traffic, such as bandwidth usage or packet loss.

In summary, network automation scripts using Go are programs that automate the management and configuration of network devices. Go is well-suited for network automation scripting due to its performance and concurrency features, and there are many libraries and frameworks available to simplify the process of writing network automation scripts. When creating network automation scripts using Go, it is important to identify the tasks that need to be automated, design scripts that can handle errors gracefully, and test the scripts thoroughly to ensure that they are working as intended.

Write, Test and Validate Automation Scripts

Here are the steps to write, test, and validate network automation scripts in Go:

Define Scope of Script

Before starting to write a network automation script, it is essential to identify the specific task that needs to be automated. This could include configuration, monitoring, or troubleshooting of network devices. Defining the scope of the script will help to determine what libraries, tools, and APIs will be needed to accomplish the task.

Install Required Libraries

Once the scope of the script has been defined, the next step is to install the required libraries, modules, and tools that will be used in the script. This could include networking libraries such as "net" or "net/http", network device management libraries such as "netconf", or SNMP libraries such as "gosnmp".

Write Codes

After installing the necessary libraries and tools, the code for the network automation script can be written. It is important to follow best practices for writing Go code, such as using package management tools like "go mod" to manage dependencies and keeping code modular and easy to read.

Test the Script

Once the code has been written, it is essential to test the script thoroughly to ensure that it is working as intended. This could involve testing the script on a test network or using virtualized network devices to simulate real-world scenarios. It is important to test the script for error handling and to ensure that it is scalable and can handle large-scale networks.

Validate the Script

Once the script has been tested, it is important to validate it by running it on a production network or on a network that is similar to the target network. This will help to ensure that the script is working correctly and that it is providing the expected results.

Iterate and Improve the Script

After validating the script, it is important to iterate and improve it based on the results of testing and validation. This could involve making changes to the code to improve performance, add new features, or to address issues that were discovered during testing or validation.

Document the Script

Finally, it is essential to document the script to ensure that it is understandable and maintainable over time. This could include adding comments to the code, creating user documentation, or writing a README file that outlines the script's purpose, dependencies, and usage instructions.

By following these steps, network engineers and administrators can create reliable and effective network automation scripts using Go. These scripts can help to streamline network management tasks, reduce errors, and save time and effort in managing complex networks.

Define Variables for Automation Scripts

Defining variables in Go is straightforward and involves the following steps:

Declare the Variable

To declare a variable in Go, you need to use the var keyword, followed by the variable name, and the data type. For example, let us declare a variable called name that will store a string:go

```go
var name string
```

Initialize the Variable

Once the variable is declared, you can initialize it with a value. This is done using the = operator, followed by the value you want to assign to the variable. For example, let us initialize the name variable to "John":

```go
var name string
name = "John"
```

You can also declare and initialize a variable in a single line of code using the := operator. For example, the following code declares and initializes the age variable to 30:

```go
age := 30
```

Use the Variable

Once the variable is declared and initialized, you can use it in your code. For example, let us print the value of the name variable to the console:

```go
fmt.Println("Name: ", name)
```

Sample Program to Define Variables

The given below is a practical demonstration of defining variables for automation scripts in Go:
let us say we want to create a script to automate the process of configuring network devices. One of the variables we'll need to define is the IP address of the device. The

given below is how we can define the variable:

```go
package main

import (
        "fmt"
)

func main() {
        var deviceIP string
        deviceIP = "192.168.1.1"

        fmt.Println("Device IP: ", deviceIP)
}
```

In the above sample program, we declared a variable called deviceIP of type string using the var keyword. We then initialized it with the IP address of the device using the = operator. Finally, we printed the value of the deviceIP variable to the console using the fmt.Println() function.

We can also declare and initialize the variable in a single line using the := operator. The given below is an updated version of the script that uses the := operator:

```go
package main

import (
        "fmt"
)

func main() {
        deviceIP := "192.168.1.1"

        fmt.Println("Device IP: ", deviceIP)
}
```

In the above sample program, we declared and initialized the deviceIP variable in a single line of code using the := operator. The result is the same as in the previous example, and we still print the value of the deviceIP variable to the console using the fmt.Println()

function.

Defining variables is a fundamental part of Go programming, and it is essential to understand how to declare, initialize, and use variables effectively in automation scripts.

Automate Configuring Host Name

To perform network automation tasks using Go, we need to use the relevant library functions and tools that are available in the Go standard library and third-party packages. The given below is a sample demonstration of how to write a script that performs network automation tasks using Go:

let us say we want to automate the process of configuring the hostname of a network device using SSH. To do this, we need to establish an SSH connection to the device, send the appropriate commands to set the hostname, and then close the connection.

Here are the steps involved in writing the code:

Import Required Packages

In this case, we need to import the golang.org/x/crypto/ssh package to establish an SSH connection and send commands to the device.

```
package main

import (
        "fmt"
        "golang.org/x/crypto/ssh"
)
```

Define Connection Parameters

We need to define the SSH connection parameters, such as the IP address, port, username, and password. We can store these values in variables to make it easier to update them in the future.

```
const (
        ip = "192.168.1.1"
        port = 22
        username = "admin"
```

```
        password = "password"
)
```

Establish SSH Connection

We can use the ssh.Dial() function to establish an SSH connection to the device.

```
config := &ssh.ClientConfig{
        User: username,
        Auth: []ssh.AuthMethod{
                ssh.Password(password),
        },
        HostKeyCallback: ssh.InsecureIgnoreHostKey(),
}

conn, err := ssh.Dial("tcp", fmt.Sprintf("%s:%d", ip, port), config)
if err != nil {
        panic(err)
}
defer conn.Close()
```

In this code, we create an SSH ClientConfig object that specifies the authentication method (in this case, password) and ignores the host key. We then use the ssh.Dial() function to connect to the device, passing in the IP address, port, and configuration object. If there's an error, we panic and terminate the program. Finally, we defer the closing of the connection until the end of the function.

Send Commands to Device

Once the connection is established, we can use the ssh.Session object to send commands to the device.

```
session, err := conn.NewSession()
if err != nil {
        panic(err)
}
defer session.Close()

commands := []string{
```

```
            "enable",
            "configure terminal",
            "hostname new-hostname",
            "end",
    }

    for _, cmd := range commands {
            err = session.Run(cmd)
            if err != nil {
                    panic(err)
            }
    }
}
```

In this code, we create a new ssh.Session object from the established connection and defer its closing until the end of the function. We then define the commands we want to send to the device in an array, and use a loop to execute each command using the session.Run() method. If there's an error executing the command, we panic and terminate the program.

Test and Validate the Code

Finally, we need to test and validate the code by running it on a test device and checking that the hostname has been successfully changed.

Putting it all together, below is the complete code for automating the process of configuring the hostname of a network device using SSH in Go:

```
package main

import (
        "fmt"
        "golang.org/x/crypto/ssh"
)

const (
        ip = "192.168.1.1"
        port = 22
        username = "admin"
```

```go
        password = "password"
)

func main() {
        config := &ssh.ClientConfig{
                User: username,
                Auth: []ssh.AuthMethod{
                        ssh.Password(password),
                HostKeyCallback: ssh.InsecureIgnoreHostKey(),
        }
}

conn, err := ssh.Dial("tcp", fmt.Sprintf("%s:%d", ip, port), config)
if err != nil {
        panic(err)
}
defer conn.Close()

session, err := conn.NewSession()
if err != nil {
        panic(err)
}
defer session.Close()

commands := []string{
        "enable",
        "configure terminal",
        "hostname new-hostname",
        "end",
}

for _, cmd := range commands {
        err = session.Run(cmd)
        if err != nil {
                panic(err)
        }
}
```

```
fmt.Println("Hostname successfully changed to 'new-hostname'")
}
```

In this code, we define the connection parameters as constants at the top of the file. We then define the `main()` function, which contains the code for establishing an SSH connection, sending the commands to set the hostname, and printing a success message.

When this code is executed, it will establish an SSH connection to the device, send the commands to set the hostname, and print a success message. If there are any errors during the process, the program will terminate and print an error message.

In summary, network automation scripts using Go can be written using the relevant library functions and tools available in the Go standard library and third-party packages. These scripts typically involve establishing a connection to a network device, sending commands to the device, and validating the results. By following the steps outlined above, we can write, test, and validate network automation scripts in Go to streamline and simplify network management tasks.

Testing Automation Script in Test Environment

Testing network automation code in Go is an important step to ensure that it is working as expected before deploying it in a production environment. There are several ways to test Go code, and in this section, we will demonstrate how to test network automation code using a test environment.

In the below sample program, we will test the code we wrote earlier to change the hostname of a network device. To test this code, we will create a test environment consisting of a virtual machine running the same operating system as the network device we want to manage. This virtual machine will be configured to simulate the network device, allowing us to run our automation code against it.
Here are the steps to create and test the code:

Set up a Test Environment

Create a virtual machine with the same operating system as the network device we want to manage.

Configure the virtual machine to simulate the network device, including setting up the necessary network interfaces and configuring the device's settings.

Install any necessary software, such as SSH or SNMP agents, to allow the device to be managed remotely.

Copy Automation Code to Test Environment

Copy the Go code we wrote earlier to the test environment, either by cloning the Git repository or by manually copying the code.

Install any necessary dependencies, such as the Go SSH library, using the Go package manager (go get).

Test the Code

Run the Go code using the go run command and verify that the hostname of the simulated device is changed as expected.

If there are any errors, debug the code using the Go debugger (dlv) or by adding logging statements to the code.

Sample Program of Testing Automation Script in Test Environment

Set up a test environment
Create a virtual machine running the same version of the Cisco IOS operating system as the network device we want to manage.
Configure the virtual machine to simulate the network device by configuring its network interfaces and settings.
Install the OpenSSH server on the virtual machine to allow remote access via SSH.

Copy the automation code to the test environment
Copy the Go code we wrote earlier to the virtual machine by cloning the Git repository using the git clone command.
Install the necessary Go SSH library by running the go get golang.org/x/crypto/ssh command.

Test the code
Run the Go code using the go run command and verify that the hostname of the

simulated device is changed as expected:

```
go run main.go -ip 192.168.1.1 -user admin -password password -port 22
```

If the code runs successfully, the output should be "Hostname successfully changed to 'new-hostname'".
If there are any errors, use the Go debugger or add logging statements to the code to identify and fix the issue.

By following these steps, we can test the network automation code using a test environment and ensure that it is working as expected before deploying it in a production environment. This approach allows us to catch any issues early and avoid potential downtime or issues with our network devices.

Debug Errors in Testing

Debugging errors or issues that arise during testing is an important part of developing network automation scripts using Go. In this section, we will demonstrate how to use the Go debugger (dlv) to debug errors in our code.

To demonstrate the debugging process, let us consider an example where we are trying to configure a network device using SSH and the configuration commands are not being applied successfully. Here are the steps to debug the issue:

Install Go Debugger

If you have not already installed the Go debugger (dlv), you can do so using the following command:

```
go get github.com/go-delve/delve/cmd/dlv
```

Add Breakpoints to Code

To debug the code, we need to set breakpoints in the code where we want the debugger to stop and allow us to inspect the program's state.

In our example, we can set breakpoints at the beginning of the function that executes the configuration commands to inspect the state of the network device and verify that the commands are being applied correctly.

We can set a breakpoint in Go using the dlv command followed by the name of the Go binary and the line number where we want the breakpoint to be set:

```
dlv debug main.go -- -ip 192.168.1.1 -user admin -password password -port 22
(dlv) break main.configureDevice
```

Run the Code with Debugger

Now that we have set our breakpoints, we can run the code with the debugger using the continue command:

```
(dlv) continue
```

Inspect Program's State

When the program hits the breakpoint, the debugger will stop and allow us to inspect the program's state.
We can inspect variables, step through the code line by line, and execute commands to modify the program's state.

In our example, we can inspect the output of the configuration commands to verify that they are being applied correctly:

```
(dlv) print output
```

Continue Execution

After we have inspected the program's state, we can continue execution using the continue command:

```
(dlv) continue
```

Repeat the previous steps 3-5 until the issue is resolved.

If there are any errors or issues with the program, we can repeat steps 3-5 to debug the issue and make any necessary changes to the code.
We can also use the help command in the debugger to see a list of available commands and their usage.

By using the Go debugger, we can easily debug errors or issues in our network automation scripts and ensure that they are working as expected. This approach allows us to catch any issues early and avoid potential downtime or issues with our network devices.

Validate Automation Scripts in Production

Validating the network automation code in Go is an important step to ensure that the code is working as expected in a production environment or on production devices. In this section, we will demonstrate how to validate our network automation code in Go by running it on a production device.

To demonstrate the validation process, let us consider an example where we are trying to automate the configuration of a network device using SSH. Here are the steps to validate our network automation code:

Prepare the Production Environment

Before we can run our code on a production device, we need to ensure that the device is set up and ready for the configuration changes that our code will make.

We can do this by checking the device configuration, verifying connectivity, and ensuring that there are no issues with the device that may cause the configuration changes to fail.

Build and Package the Code

Once we have validated the production environment, we can build and package our code into a binary that can be run on the production device.

We can do this by running the go build command followed by the name of the main package:
go build main.go

This will create a binary file with the same name as the package in the current directory.

Copy Binary to Production Device

After we have built the binary, we need to copy it to the production device.

We can do this using tools like scp or rsync to securely transfer the binary to the device over SSH:

scp main user@192.168.1.1:/home/user/

Run the Code on Production Device

Once the binary has been copied to the production device, we can run it on the device to configure the device.

We can do this by logging into the device over SSH and running the binary:

```
ssh user@192.168.1.1
./main -ip 192.168.1.1 -user admin -password password -port 22
```

Verify the Configuration Changes

After running the code, we should verify that the configuration changes have been applied correctly.

We can do this by checking the device configuration, verifying connectivity, and ensuring that there are no issues with the device that may cause the configuration changes to fail.

Repeat Steps 1-5 for Each Device

If we have multiple devices that we want to configure, we should repeat steps 1-5 for each device to ensure that our code is working as expected on all devices.

By following these steps, we can validate our network automation code in Go and ensure that it is working as expected on production devices. This approach allows us to catch any issues early and avoid potential downtime or issues with our network devices.

Summary

In this chapter, we have discussed the steps involved in writing, testing, and validating network automation scripts using Go. Network automation scripts are used to automate the configuration of network devices such as routers, switches, and firewalls. By automating these tasks, network administrators can save time and reduce the risk of human error.

To write network automation scripts in Go, we first need to define the variables that we will be using in the script. These variables could include things like IP addresses, usernames, passwords, and commands to be executed on the device. We can define these variables using the var keyword or using command-line arguments.

Once we have defined the variables, we can write the code that will perform the necessary network automation tasks using the library functions and tools of Go. This could include opening an SSH session, executing commands on the device, and parsing the output to extract the necessary information.

After we have written the code, we need to test it to ensure that it is working as expected. We can do this by running the code on a test environment or test devices. During testing, we should look out for any errors or issues that may arise and fix them as needed.

If there are any errors or issues that we are unable to fix during testing, we can use debugging tools like panic, recover, and defer to help us identify and fix the issues.

Once we are satisfied that our code is working correctly, we can validate it by running it on the production environment or devices. To do this, we need to prepare the production environment, build and package the code, copy the binary to the production device, and run the code on the device. We should then verify that the configuration changes have been applied correctly and repeat the process for each device.

Overall, writing, testing, and validating network automation scripts in Go requires a solid understanding of the programming language, networking concepts, and the specific devices and environments that we are working with. By following these steps and best practices, we can automate network tasks with confidence and reduce the risk of human error.

CHAPTER 5:
AUTOMATION OF
CONFIGURATION
MANAGEMENT

Neccessity of Configuration Management

Overview

Configuration management is the process of managing and controlling the configurations of software and hardware systems. In the context of IT infrastructure, configuration management involves managing the configuration of network devices, servers, and other IT assets. The purpose of configuration management is to ensure that these systems are always in the desired state and to facilitate easy recovery in case of a failure.

Configuration management is a crucial aspect of IT operations because it helps to ensure the stability, availability, and security of IT systems. By keeping track of all changes made to a system, configuration management enables administrators to easily revert to a previous state if something goes wrong. Additionally, configuration management helps to reduce the risk of configuration drift, which occurs when systems deviate from their intended configuration over time due to manual changes, updates, or other factors.

Benefits of Configuration Management

There are several benefits of implementing configuration management in an IT environment. Firstly, configuration management helps to improve efficiency by automating routine tasks and reducing the need for manual intervention. This allows IT staff to focus on more important tasks such as problem-solving and strategic planning.

Secondly, configuration management helps to improve consistency across the IT environment. By ensuring that all systems are configured in the same way, configuration management helps to reduce the risk of errors and inconsistencies that can arise when systems are configured manually.

Thirdly, configuration management helps to improve security by enabling administrators to quickly detect and respond to security incidents. By keeping track of all changes made to a system, configuration management makes it easier to identify and remediate security vulnerabilities.

Finally, configuration management helps to improve compliance with industry standards and regulations. By keeping track of all changes made to a system and ensuring that systems are configured in a consistent and secure manner, configuration management enables organizations to demonstrate compliance with relevant standards and regulations.

While configuration management can be done manually, automating it with Go can bring several benefits. Go is a fast, efficient, and powerful programming language that is well-suited for automating configuration management tasks. By using Go to automate configuration management, administrators can improve efficiency, reduce the risk of errors and inconsistencies, and improve security.

Role of Go in Configuration Management

Some of the specific benefits of using Go for configuration management include:

Efficiency: Go's simple and concise syntax makes it easy to write automation scripts that are efficient and performant. This enables administrators to automate routine tasks and free up time for more important tasks.

Cross-platform support: Go's cross-platform support makes it easy to write automation scripts that can be run on multiple operating systems and architectures. This helps to ensure that configuration management is consistent across the entire IT environment.

Concurrency: Go's support for concurrency makes it easy to write automation scripts that can perform multiple tasks simultaneously. This enables administrators to automate complex tasks that would be difficult or time-consuming to perform manually.

Testing: Go's built-in testing support makes it easy to write unit tests and integration tests for automation scripts. This helps to ensure that scripts are working correctly and reduces the risk of errors and inconsistencies.

Integration with other tools: Go can easily integrate with other tools and frameworks such as Ansible, Terraform, and Kubernetes. This enables administrators to build comprehensive automation workflows that span multiple tools and environments.

Overall, implementing configuration management and automating it with Go can bring several benefits to IT operations. By ensuring that systems are always in the desired state, configuration management helps to improve efficiency, consistency, security, and compliance. By using Go to automate configuration management tasks, administrators can take advantage of Go's speed, efficiency, and powerful features to streamline IT operations and reduce the risk of errors and inconsistencies.

Server Provisioning with Puppet and Go

Server provisioning is the process of setting up a server with the necessary hardware, software, and configurations to make it ready for use. This process involves a series of tasks such as installing the operating system, configuring network settings, installing and configuring software packages, setting up security measures, and more.

Puppet is a popular configuration management tool that can automate the process of server provisioning. It uses a declarative language to define the desired state of a server, and then automatically configures the server to match that state.

To use Puppet with Go, you first need to install Puppet and configure it to work with your servers. Once you have done this, you can write Puppet code to automate your server provisioning process. let us look at an example.

Suppose you want to provision a server with the Apache web server and configure it to serve a basic HTML page. Here are the steps you would take:

Install Puppet on Server(s)

Write a Puppet manifest to define the desired state of the server. In this case, the manifest would include code to install the Apache package and create a basic HTML file. The given below is an example:

```
package { 'apache2':
  ensure => installed,
}

file { '/var/www/html/index.html':
  ensure  => file,
  content => '<html><body><h1>Hello, world!</h1></body></html>',
}
```

This manifest uses Puppet's built-in resource types to install the Apache package and create a file at /var/www/html/index.html with the specified content.

Apply Puppet Manifest to Server(s)

This will automatically install the Apache package and create the HTML file. To apply the manifest, you can use the puppet apply command:

```
sudo puppet apply /path/to/manifest.pp
```

Verify that the server is provisioned correctly. You can do this by accessing the server's IP address in a web browser and checking that the "Hello, world!" message is displayed.

By using Puppet and Go together, you can automate your server provisioning process and ensure that your servers are always configured to your desired state. This can save you time and reduce the risk of errors or inconsistencies in your server configurations.

Additionally, Puppet provides a number of other benefits for server management and configuration, such as:

- Configuration consistency: With Puppet, you can define the desired state of your servers once and then apply that configuration consistently across all of your servers.
- Version control: Puppet code can be version-controlled using tools like Git, allowing you to track changes and revert to previous versions if necessary.
- Auditing and reporting: Puppet provides tools for tracking changes to your server configurations and generating reports on your server infrastructure.

In summary, server provisioning is the process of setting up a server with the necessary hardware, software, and configurations to make it ready for use. Puppet is a popular configuration management tool that can automate this process using a declarative language. By using Puppet and Go together, you can automate your server provisioning process and ensure that your servers are always configured to your desired state. This can save you time, reduce the risk of errors, and provide other benefits for server management and configuration.

Automation of System Settings

Let us see an example of how to automate system settings using Go.

In the below sample program, we will automate the process of setting the timezone of a Linux system to "America/Los_Angeles" using the Go programming language.

Importing Necessary Packages

The first step is to import the necessary packages to interact with the operating system and modify system settings. In this case, we will use the "os/exec" package to execute shell commands and the "log" package for logging.

```
package main

import (
    "log"
    "os/exec"
)
```

Defining Function to Set Timezone

Next, we will define a function that sets the timezone of the system using the "timedatectl" command.

```
func setTimeZone() error {
    cmd := exec.Command("timedatectl", "set-timezone", "America/Los_Angeles")
    err := cmd.Run()
    if err != nil {
        return err
    }
    log.Println("Timezone set to America/Los_Angeles")
    return nil
}
```

This function creates a new command using the "timedatectl" command with the argument "set-timezone" and the timezone string "America/Los_Angeles". It then executes the command using the "Run" method of the "cmd" object. If there is an error during execution, it returns the error. Otherwise, it logs a message indicating that the timezone has been set and returns nil.

Calling the Function

Finally, we will call the "setTimeZone" function in the "main" function of our program.

```
func main() {
    err := setTimeZone()
    if err != nil {
        log.Fatal(err)
    }
}
```

This calls the "setTimeZone" function and checks if there is an error. If there is an error, it logs the error message and exits the program using the "Fatal" function of the "log" package.

Building and Running the Program

To build and run the program, we can use the following commands:

```
go build
./example-program
```

This will build the program and execute it, which will set the timezone to "America/Los_Angeles" and log a message indicating that the timezone has been set.

Automating the Process

To automate this process, we can use a configuration management tool like Puppet to run this script on multiple systems. We can create a Puppet module that includes this script and applies it to all nodes that require the timezone setting.

For example, we can create a Puppet module called "timezone" with a manifest file that includes the following code:

```
class timezone {
  exec { "set_timezone":
    command => "/path/to/example-program",
  }
}
```

This defines a Puppet class called "timezone" that includes an "exec" resource that runs the "example-program" script.

When we apply this Puppet module to our nodes, it will automatically set the timezone to "America/Los_Angeles" on all systems that require it.

In summary, automating system settings using Go can help save time and effort when configuring multiple systems. By defining functions that interact with the operating system and creating Puppet modules that include these functions, we can automate the process of configuring system settings and ensure that they are consistent across all nodes.

Modify Base Configurations

Base configurations are the fundamental configuration settings that are applied to all devices in a network or a specific group of devices. These configurations are the backbone of the network and typically include things like firewall rules, routing protocols, and other basic network settings that are essential for the network to function properly.

Modifying base configurations with Go is a straightforward process that involves writing a script to make the necessary changes and applying them to the devices in question. Below is a sample demonstration of how this can be done:

Identify Base Configurations to Modify

Before we can begin modifying the base configurations, we need to identify what needs to be changed. This might involve reviewing the existing configurations, consulting with network administrators or engineers, or conducting a network audit to determine where improvements can be made.

Write the Go Script

Once we know what needs to be modified, we can begin writing the Go script to make those changes. Below is an example of what that script might look like:

```go
package main

import (
        "fmt"
        "log"
        "os/exec"
)

func main() {
        // Open the configuration file for editing
        cmd := exec.Command("nano", "/etc/network/interfaces")
        err := cmd.Run()
        if err != nil {
                log.Fatal(err)
        }

        // Restart the network service to apply the changes
        cmd = exec.Command("service", "networking", "restart")
        err = cmd.Run()
        if err != nil {
                log.Fatal(err)
        }
```

```
        fmt.Println("Base configurations modified successfully!")
}
```

This script uses the os/exec package to execute two shell commands: one to open the network interfaces configuration file for editing, and another to restart the network service to apply the changes. Of course, the exact commands used will depend on the specific base configurations being modified.

Apply the Changes

Once the script has been written and saved, we can run it on the devices in question to modify the base configurations. This might involve using a tool like Puppet to automate the process across multiple devices at once.

Below is an example of how to modify base configurations using Puppet and the Go script we just created:

```
node 'webserver' {
  exec { 'modify_base_config':
    command => '/usr/local/bin/modify_base_config',
    require => Package['go'],
  }
}
```

This Puppet manifest tells the 'webserver' node to execute the modify_base_config script located at /usr/local/bin/modify_base_config. The require attribute ensures that the go package is installed before running the script.

Verify the Changes

Finally, we need to verify that the changes have been applied correctly. This might involve reviewing the configuration files to ensure that the desired modifications have been made, running network tests to ensure that the changes have not caused any issues, and monitoring the network to ensure that everything is functioning as expected.

To summarize, modifying base configurations is an essential part of network management, and doing it with Go can greatly simplify the process. By writing scripts to automate the modification process and using tools like Puppet to apply those changes across multiple devices, we can ensure that our network is properly configured and functioning as it should be.

Automating System Identification

Automating system identification can help streamline the process of configuring and managing systems in a network. Combining Go and Puppet together can be an effective way to achieve this automation. In this section, we will discuss the steps to automate system identification using Go and Puppet.

Install Puppet and Go

First, we need to install Puppet and Go on the system. Puppet is a configuration management tool that can help us automate system configuration, while Go is a programming language that we can use to write automation scripts. We can download and install both of these tools from their official websites.

Define Puppet Manifests

Next, we need to define the Puppet manifests that we will use to configure our systems. A manifest is a file that contains the configuration code for Puppet. We can create a new manifest file in a text editor and give it a name such as "system_identification.pp". We can then add code to the file to define the system identification settings we want to apply to our systems.

For example, we can use the following Puppet code to set the hostname of our systems:

```
node 'webserver' {
  class { 'hostname':
    hostname => 'webserver.local',
  }
}
```

This code defines a Puppet class called "hostname" and sets the hostname of the system to "webserver.local" for the node named "webserver".

Write Go Scripts

Next, we need to write Go scripts that will execute our Puppet manifests on the target systems. We can use the Go Puppet API to interact with Puppet and apply our manifests.

We can create a new Go file in a text editor and give it a name such as "system_identification.go". We can then import the necessary Go and Puppet packages and define our Go script.

For example, we can use the following Go code to apply our Puppet manifest:

```go
package main

import (
        "fmt"
        "os"

        "github.com/puppetlabs/puppet-go/puppet"
)

func main() {
        // Create a new Puppet client
        client, err := puppet.NewClient(puppet.ClientOptions{
                CACertFile:  "/etc/puppetlabs/puppet/ssl/ca/ca_crt.pem",
                CertFile:    "/etc/puppetlabs/puppet/ssl/certs/client.crt",
                KeyFile:     "/etc/puppetlabs/puppet/ssl/private_keys/client.pem",
                MasterURL:   "puppet://puppet-master.example.com",
                NodeName:    "webserver",
                Environment: "production",
                ReportFormat: "yaml",
        })
        if err != nil {
                fmt.Fprintf(os.Stderr, "Failed to create Puppet client: %v\n", err)
                os.Exit(1)
        }

        // Apply the system identification manifest
        err = client.Apply("system_identification.pp")
        if err != nil {
                fmt.Fprintf(os.Stderr, "Failed to apply system identification manifest: %v\n", err)
                os.Exit(1)
        }
```

```
        fmt.Println("System identification complete!")
}
```

This code defines a main function that creates a new Puppet client with the necessary configuration options. It then calls the client's Apply function to apply our "system_identification.pp" manifest to the target system. Finally, it prints a message indicating that the system identification is complete.

Run the Go Script

Finally, we need to run our Go script to apply our Puppet manifest to the target system. We can compile and run our script using the following commands:

```
$ go build system_identification.go
$ sudo ./system_identification
System identification complete!
```

This will compile and run our Go script, which will apply our Puppet manifest and set the hostname of the target system

Automating System Patches and Updates

System patches and updates are critical to ensure that the system remains secure and up-to-date with the latest features and functionalities. However, manually patching and updating every system can be a tedious and time-consuming process. This is where automation comes in handy.

In this demonstration, we will show how to use Go and Puppet to automate system patches and updates. Puppet is a popular configuration management tool that helps to automate repetitive tasks. It provides a declarative language to describe the desired state of the system, and Puppet takes care of ensuring that the system is in that desired state.

Create New Directory for Project

```
mkdir patching-project
cd patching-project
```

Initialize New Go Module in Directory

go mod init patching-project

Create New Go File 'main.go' and Import Necessary Packages

package main

```go
import (
    "fmt"
    "os/exec"
)

func main() {
    // Update the package lists
    cmd := exec.Command("sudo", "apt-get", "update")
    err := cmd.Run()
    if err != nil {
        fmt.Println("Error updating package lists:", err)
        return
    }

    // Upgrade the packages
    cmd = exec.Command("sudo", "apt-get", "upgrade", "-y")
    err = cmd.Run()
    if err != nil {
        fmt.Println("Error upgrading packages:", err)
        return
    }

    fmt.Println("System is up-to-date.")
}
```

This Go code will run the sudo apt-get update and sudo apt-get upgrade -y commands to update and upgrade the system packages.

Create Puppet Manifest 'patching.pp' to Manage Go Code

```
class patching {
  exec { "patching":
    command => "go run /path/to/main.go",
  }
}
```

This Puppet manifest will run the Go code as a Puppet exec resource. The command attribute specifies the command to run, which is the go run /path/to/main.go command.

Apply the Puppet Manifest

sudo puppet apply patching.pp

This command will apply the patching.pp manifest, which will execute the Go code to patch and update the system.

You have now automated system patches and updates using Go and Puppet. In conclusion, automating system patches and updates is essential to ensure system security and functionality. Go and Puppet provide an easy and effective way to automate these tasks, which can save time and effort in the long run.

Identifying Unstable and Non-compliant Configuration

Identifying unstable and non-compliant configurations is an important part of configuration management. It helps ensure that all systems are operating according to the organization's standards and best practices, and it can help prevent security vulnerabilities and downtime.

One way to identify unstable and non-compliant configurations is by using configuration auditing tools. These tools scan systems and compare their configurations against a set of predefined policies and rules, highlighting any discrepancies or violations.

In this demonstration, we will use the popular open-source tool "InSpec" to identify unstable and non-compliant configurations in our system. InSpec is a configuration auditing and compliance tool that allows you to define policies and rules in a simple and human-readable format.

Here are the steps to automate the process of identifying unstable and non-compliant configurations using Go and InSpec:

Install InSpec

First, we need to install InSpec on our system. InSpec can be installed on various platforms such as Linux, Windows, and macOS. In this demonstration, we will install InSpec on a Linux-based system. The installation instructions can be found on the InSpec website.

Create an InSpec Profile

Next, we need to create an InSpec profile. An InSpec profile is a collection of rules and policies that define the desired configuration of a system. We can create an InSpec profile using the "inspec init profile" command.

```
$ inspec init profile my-profile
```

This command creates a new InSpec profile named "my-profile" in the current directory.

Define Policies and Rules

Once we have created an InSpec profile, we can define policies and rules that check for unstable and non-compliant configurations. In this demonstration, we will define a simple policy that checks whether the root account has a password set.

```
my-profile/controls/root.rb
control 'root-password' do
impact 1.0
title 'Root password must be set'
desc 'The root account should have a password set to prevent unauthorized access'
describe shadow.users('root').passwords.first.password_hash do
it { should_not eq '*' }
end
end
```

This policy checks whether the root account's password hash is set to "" in the "/etc/shadow" file. If the password hash is "", it means that the root account does not have a password set, which is a security risk.

Run InSpec Audit

Once we have defined our policies and rules, we can run an InSpec audit to check for unstable and non-compliant configurations. We can do this using the "inspec exec" command.

$ inspec exec my-profile

This command runs the "my-profile" InSpec profile and generates a report of any discrepancies or violations.

Integrate with Go

Finally, we can integrate this process with our Go automation script. We can use the "exec.Command" function to execute the "inspec exec" command and capture its output.

```
package main

import (
"fmt"
"os/exec"
)

func main() {
cmd := exec.Command("inspec", "exec", "my-profile")
out, err := cmd.CombinedOutput()
if err != nil {
fmt.Println("Error:", err)
}
fmt.Println(string(out))
}
```

This code runs the "inspec exec" command and captures its output. If there are any violations, they will be printed to the console.

InSpec provides a simple and effective way to identify unstable and non-compliant configurations in your system. By integrating InSpec with Go, we can automate this process and ensure that our systems are always configured according to our organization's policies and rules.

Summary

In this chapter, we discussed configuration management and the benefits of automating it using Go. Configuration management is the process of managing changes to an IT system's software, hardware, and networking configurations to ensure that they are consistent, accurate, and up-to-date. By automating configuration management, organizations can reduce the time and effort required to manage systems and minimize errors and inconsistencies.

Server provisioning is the process of setting up new servers with the required software, configurations, and resources. We demonstrated how to use Puppet to provision a new server with Go, which can automate the process and ensure that new servers are set up consistently and accurately.

We also discussed automating system settings, which involves automating the configuration of various system settings, such as network settings, user accounts, and firewall rules. We demonstrated how to use Go to automate system settings by writing code that can update and configure these settings automatically.

Modifying base configurations is the process of modifying the base configurations of a system to meet specific requirements. We demonstrated how to modify base configurations using Go, and optionally, using Puppet. This can ensure that systems are configured correctly and consistently across the organization.

Automating system identification involves automatically identifying the configuration of systems in the organization, including hardware, software, and network configurations. We demonstrated how to combine Go and Puppet to automate system identification and ensure that systems are correctly identified and classified.

Automating system patches and updates involves automatically applying updates and patches to systems to ensure that they are secure and up-to-date. We demonstrated how to use Go to automate system updates and patches, which can reduce the risk of vulnerabilities and ensure that systems are secure.

Finally, we discussed identifying unstable and non-compliant configurations, which involves identifying configurations that do not meet organizational standards or that are unstable. We demonstrated how to use Go and Puppet to identify and remediate unstable configurations automatically.

Overall, automation of configuration management, server provisioning, system settings, base configurations, system identification, updates, and patches, and identifying unstable configurations using Go can help organizations ensure that their systems are consistent, accurate, and up-to-date. It can also reduce the time and effort required to manage systems and minimize errors and inconsistencies.

CHAPTER 6: NETWORKING WITH CONTAINER AND DOCKER

Understanding Docker and Containers

Overview

Docker is an open-source containerization platform used to create, deploy and manage applications in a containerized environment. A container is a lightweight and standalone executable package that contains all the dependencies and libraries required to run the application. Docker containers provide a portable and efficient way to run applications across different platforms and environments.

Containers are isolated from the host system and other containers, which makes them more secure and reliable than traditional virtual machines. Docker containers are based on images, which are read-only templates that contain the application code, dependencies, and libraries required to run the application.

Role of Go in Containerization

Go networking plays a significant role in the Docker ecosystem. Go is the primary language used to develop Docker and is used to create and manage networking components of Docker. Go is a high-performance language that provides efficient networking capabilities, making it a perfect fit for the Docker networking layer.

The Docker networking model is designed to provide connectivity between containers and external networks, such as the internet or a local network. The Docker networking model provides a range of networking options, including bridge networks, overlay networks, host networks, and macvlan networks.

Bridge networks are the default networking mode in Docker and provide connectivity between containers on the same host. Bridge networks use a virtual Ethernet bridge to connect containers to the host network. Each container is assigned a unique IP address within the bridge network.

Overlay networks are used to connect containers running on different hosts. Overlay networks use a VXLAN tunnel to provide connectivity between containers on different hosts. Overlay networks provide a virtual network overlay on top of the physical network infrastructure.

Host networks allow containers to use the network stack of the host system directly. This networking mode provides the highest performance and lowest latency but reduces isolation between containers.

Macvlan networks allow containers to use a physical network interface of the host system directly. This networking mode provides better network isolation than host networks but can be more complex to set up.

Go networking is used to create and manage these networking components of Docker. The Go standard library provides a range of networking packages, including net, net/http, and net/rpc, which are used extensively in Docker.

The net package provides a range of functions and types for working with TCP/IP networks. The net/http package provides functions for creating HTTP clients and servers. The net/rpc package provides functions for creating RPC clients and servers.

Go networking is also used to manage the lifecycle of containers in Docker. The Docker API provides a range of networking endpoints, which can be used to create, inspect, and manage networking components of Docker.

To create a container with a specific network configuration, we can use the Docker CLI or the Docker API. For example, to create a container with a bridge network, we can use the following Docker CLI command:

```
docker run --network=bridge -d nginx
```

This command creates a new container running the nginx image and connects it to the default bridge network.

In addition to the Docker networking model, Go networking is used extensively in container orchestration platforms such as Kubernetes. Kubernetes uses Go networking to create and manage networking components such as services, load balancers, and ingress controllers.

To summarize, Go networking plays a crucial role in the Docker ecosystem by providing efficient networking capabilities for containerized applications. The Docker networking model provides a range of networking options, including bridge networks, overlay networks, host networks, and macvlan networks. Go networking is used to create and manage these networking components of Docker, and the Go standard library provides a range of networking packages for working with TCP/IP networks, HTTP clients and servers, and RPC clients and servers.

Installing Docker

First, ensure that your server meets the minimum system requirements for running Docker.

You can find the system requirements on the Docker documentation website.

Next, you'll need to install Docker on your server. You can do this by running the following command:

```
curl -fsSL https://get.docker.com -o get-docker.sh
sudo sh get-docker.sh
```

This will download and install Docker on your server.

Once Docker is installed, you'll need to create a Docker network for Go to use. You can do this by running the following command:

```
docker network create go-network
```

This will create a Docker network called "go-network".

Now that the Docker network is set up, you can start a new Docker container for your Go application. To do this, you'll first need to create a Dockerfile for your application. The given below is an example Dockerfile:

```
FROM golang:latest
WORKDIR /app
COPY . .
RUN go build -o main .
CMD ["./main"]
```

This Dockerfile sets up a container based on the latest version of the official Go image, sets the working directory to /app, copies the contents of the current directory into the container, builds the Go application, and then runs the resulting executable.

Once you've created your Dockerfile, you can build a Docker image for your application by running the following command in the same directory as the Dockerfile:

```
docker build -t my-go-app .
```

This will build a Docker image named "my-go-app" based on the instructions in your Dockerfile.

Finally, you can start a new Docker container for your Go application using the following command:

```
docker run --name my-go-container --network go-network -p 8080:8080 -d my-
go-app
```

This will start a new Docker container named "my-go-container" using the "my-go-app" Docker image you just built. The container will be connected to the "go-network" Docker network, and it will be accessible on port 8080 on your server.

Building Docker Images

Docker images are the basic building blocks of Docker containers. They are essentially pre-packaged, read-only templates that contain all the necessary files and dependencies required to run a specific application or service inside a container. Docker images are created using a Dockerfile, which is a text file that contains instructions for building the image. In this section, we will discuss how to build a Docker image practically using Go.

To build a Docker image, we need to follow these steps:

Install Docker

First, we need to install Docker on our machine. Docker provides installation packages for different operating systems, which can be downloaded from their website.

Create a Dockerfile

Next, we need to create a Dockerfile that contains instructions for building the Docker image. The Dockerfile contains a set of instructions that define the base image, the dependencies to be installed, the application code, and the commands to be run when the container is started.

Below is an example Dockerfile for building a Docker image for a simple Go web application:

```
# Set the base image
FROM golang:1.16

# Set the working directory
WORKDIR /app

# Copy the source code to the working directory
COPY . .
```

```
# Build the Go application
RUN go build -o app .

# Expose port 8080 for the application
EXPOSE 8080

# Set the command to run the application
CMD [ "./app" ]
```

This Dockerfile sets the base image to the official Go image, copies the source code to the working directory, builds the Go application, exposes port 8080 for the application, and sets the command to run the application.

Build the Docker Image

Once the Dockerfile is created, we can use the docker build command to build the Docker image. The docker build command takes the path to the directory containing the Dockerfile and builds the image based on the instructions in the Dockerfile.

Below is an example command to build the Docker image for the above Dockerfile:

```
docker build -t my-go-app .
```

The -t flag is used to specify the name and tag for the Docker image, and the . specifies the path to the directory containing the Dockerfile.

Verify the Docker Image

Once the Docker image is built, we can use the docker images command to verify that the image has been created.
Below is an example command to verify the Docker image:

```
docker images
```

This command will list all the Docker images on the machine, including the newly built image.

By following these steps, we can build a Docker image for our Go application. Once the image is built, we can use it to create and run containers for our application.

Running Containers

To begin with, we will first ensure that Docker is installed and running on your system. You can confirm this by running the following command in your terminal:

docker --version

Assuming Docker is properly installed and running, we can proceed with creating a Docker image and running a container.

Create a Go Program

```
package main

import (
    "fmt"
    "time"
)

func main() {
    fmt.Println("Starting the Go program...")

    for i := 1; i <= 5; i++ {
        fmt.Printf("Processing step %d\n", i)
        time.Sleep(1 * time.Second)
    }

    fmt.Println("Exiting the Go program.")
}
```

Build the Docker Image using Dockerfile

```
FROM golang:1.16

WORKDIR /go/src/app
COPY . .
```

```
RUN go get -d -v ./...
RUN go install -v ./...

CMD ["app"]
```

You can build the Docker image by running the following command in the terminal:

```
docker build -t my-go-app .
```

This will create a Docker image named my-go-app using the Dockerfile.

Run the Docker Container

```
docker run my-go-app
```

This will run the Docker container using the my-go-app image. You should see the output from the Go program in your terminal.

You can also run the Docker container in detached mode using the -d flag:

```
docker run -d my-go-app
```

To see a list of running Docker containers, use the following command:

```
docker ps
```

To stop a running Docker container, use the following command:

```
docker stop <container_id>
```

In summary, the above steps demonstrate how to run a simple Go program in a Docker container. You can customize this process to fit your specific needs and applications.

Automate Container Operations

To automate the running of containers, we can use tools like Docker Compose, which allows us to define multi-container applications and their dependencies in a single configuration file.

Here are the steps to automate the running of containers using Docker Compose and Go:

Install Docker and Docker Compose

Before we can start using Docker Compose, we need to have Docker and Docker Compose installed on our system. We can follow the installation instructions provided by the Docker documentation.

Define the Container Configurations

Next, we need to define the container configurations in a Docker Compose file, which is a YAML file that describes the services, networks, and volumes required for our application. Below is an example Docker Compose file that defines two containers - one for a Go web server and another for a MySQL database:

```
version: '3'

services:
  web:
    build: .
    ports:
      - "8080:8080"
    depends_on:
      - db
  db:
    image: mysql:5.7
    environment:
      MYSQL_ROOT_PASSWORD: example
```

In the below sample program, we have defined two services - web and db. The web service builds a Docker image from the current directory (which contains our Go web server code), maps port 8080 on the container to port 8080 on the host, and depends on the db service. The db service uses the mysql:5.7 image and sets the MYSQL_ROOT_PASSWORD environment variable to example.

Build and Start the Containers

Once we have defined our Docker Compose file, we can use the docker-compose command to build and start our containers. From the directory containing our Docker Compose file, we can run the following command:

docker-compose up

This will build the Docker image for the web service (if it hasn't already been built), start both the web and db containers, and stream their output to the console.

Test the Running Containers

Once our containers are running, we can test them to ensure that they are working correctly. In the below sample program, we can test our Go web server by opening a web browser and navigating to http://localhost:8080. If everything is working correctly, we should see a webpage served by our Go web server.

We can also use the docker-compose ps command to view the status of our containers and their ports.

Stop and Remove the Containers

When we are done using our containers, we can stop and remove them using the following command:

docker-compose down

This will stop and remove the running containers and their associated resources.

By using Docker and Docker Compose to automate the running of containers, we can easily manage and deploy our applications, while also taking advantage of Go's powerful networking features.

Managing Container Networks

Need of Container Networking

Managing container networks is an important aspect of using Docker and other container technologies. Container networking allows different containers to communicate with each other and with the outside world. By default, containers can communicate with each other using an internal network created by Docker, but this may not always be sufficient. In this case, it becomes necessary to create custom networks for specific use cases.

Managing Containers using Docker CLI

In Docker, networks can be created and managed using the Docker CLI or through Docker

Compose. The given below is a practical demonstration of how to manage container networks using the Docker CLI:

List the existing networks by running the following command:

docker network ls

Create a new custom network using the following command:

docker network create --driver bridge my-network

In the above sample program, we created a new network named my-network using the bridge driver. The bridge driver is the default driver for Docker, and it provides automatic IP address assignment to containers on the network.

Verify that the new network has been created by running the following command:

ocker network ls

The output should include the newly created network.

Create a new container on the custom network using the following command:

docker run --name my-container --network my-network -d nginx

In the above sample program, we created a new container named my-container and connected it to the my-network network. The -d flag runs the container in detached mode, which means it will run in the background.

Verify that the container is running by running the following command:

docker ps

The output should include the newly created container.

Connect to the running container by running the following command:

docker exec -it my-container /bin/bash

This will open a Bash shell inside the container, allowing you to interact with it.

Verify that the container can access the internet by running the following command inside the container:

curl http://www.google.com

This should output the HTML of the Google homepage.

Disconnect from the container by typing exit.

Stop and remove the container by running the following command:

docker stop my-container && docker rm my-container

This will stop and remove the container we created earlier.

Remove the custom network by running the following command:
docker network rm my-network

This will remove the custom network we created earlier.

And that's it! By creating and managing custom networks, you can easily control how containers communicate with each other and with the outside world.

Summary

In this chapter, we discussed Docker and its role in containerization. We first started by understanding what Docker is and its concept of containerization, which allows applications to run in isolated environments. We also discussed the benefits of using Docker, such as consistency, scalability, and portability.

Next, we moved on to practical steps for installing Docker and configuring it for Go. The steps included installing Docker and its dependencies, configuring Docker to allow non-root users, and testing the installation with a simple "Hello World" program.

We then discussed Docker images and how they are used to package applications and dependencies. We covered the steps for building a Docker image using a Dockerfile, which is a text file that contains instructions for building the image. We also discussed best practices for building Docker images, such as using a minimal base image and cleaning up after each step.

After building the Docker image, we moved on to running containers. We demonstrated how to run a container using the "docker run" command and how to specify options such as the container name, network settings, and environment variables. We also discussed how to view running containers and how to stop and remove them.

To automate the running of containers, we discussed the use of Docker Compose, which is a tool for defining and running multi-container Docker applications. We demonstrated how to define a Docker Compose file that specifies the services to be run and their dependencies, and how to use the "docker-compose up" command to start the containers.

We also discussed the importance of managing container networks and how it can be done practically. We explained how container networks allow containers to communicate with each other and with external networks. We demonstrated how to create and manage container networks using the "docker network" command, and how to specify network settings in Docker Compose files.

In summary, this chapter covered various aspects of Docker and containerization, starting from its concept, benefits, installation, configuration, Docker images, running containers, automation, and managing container networks. By following the practical demonstrations provided, users can get a better understanding of how to use Docker and Go to containerize and manage their applications efficiently.

CHAPTER 7: ORCHESTRATING CONTAINERS AND AUTOMATING WORKLOADS

Networking for Container Workloads

Understanding Container Scheduling

The process of deploying, administering, and scaling containerized applications across a cluster of servers is referred to as container scheduling. It enables the effective use of computer resources by automating the placement of container workloads on various nodes, taking into account both the available resources and the requirements of the job. When it comes to handling large-scale container deployments, the scheduling process is absolutely essential. In order to guarantee high availability and performance, you need a solution that is resilient, reliable, and scalable.

Container Scheduling Techniques

Static scheduling, dynamic scheduling, and hybrid scheduling are the three primary classifications of accessible container scheduling techniques.

The static scheduling method is a straightforward strategy that assigns a fixed number of containers to each node in the cluster, independent of the demands that are placed on the cluster by the workload. It is simple to put into action, but it can lead to inefficient use of resources, which would result in higher expenses and lower performance.

The dynamic scheduling method, on the other hand, is a more insightful strategy that assigns containers according to the available resources and the workload demands. It provides optimal resource usage by dynamically scaling container workloads up or down based on demand, which makes it possible to save time and effort. This strategy calls for a more sophisticated scheduling system, but it ultimately leads to higher performance as well as more effective use of available resources.

A hybrid scheduling technique is a blend of both static and dynamic scheduling approaches. It enables administrators to assign fixed resources to particular workloads while also providing dynamic resource allocation for other workloads. This strategy grants flexibility and control over the allocation of resources, while at the same time enabling dynamic scaling.

Role of Networking Automation for Containers

By enabling the effective configuration and maintenance of container networks, network automation is an essential component of the container workload automation process. The process of container networking is a complicated one that requires the use of various layers of network abstraction. These layers include virtual networks, overlay networks, and physical networks.

Network automation solutions make it possible to deploy and scale container workloads across a cluster of servers in an effective manner. This is accomplished by automating the configuration and maintenance of container networks. This automation makes it possible for administrators to concentrate on higher-level responsibilities, such as the development and delivery of applications, while still ensuring that the underlying network infrastructure is optimal for both performance and scalability.

In addition, network automation tools like as Go networking give a variety of capabilities that make it easier to manage container networks. These functions, which include network segmentation, load balancing, and security, are all included in the tool's feature set. These characteristics make it possible for administrators to design complicated network topologies that are able to support large-scale container deployments while also ensuring excellent availability and performance.

To summarize, container scheduling is an essential part of container workload automation. This component enables the effective utilisation of computing resources while also maintaining high availability and performance. Network automation is an essential component of this process because it facilitates the effective configuration and maintenance of container networks, reduces the complexity of network topologies, and ensures high performance and scalability.

Service Discovery

Service discovery is the process of automatically discovering new services within a networked system and determining their location. It is becoming increasingly necessary for networking experts to have the capability to find new services in an automated manner as networks continue to get more complex and dynamic. With service discovery, managers are able to easily scale up or down their infrastructure without having to manually configure new servers or update old ones. This saves them time and reduces the risk of human error. In addition to this, it helps to ensure that services are available and can communicate with each other without any interruptions, which improves the overall dependability and performance of the system.

Discovery of services can be carried out in a number of different ways, including discovery that is based on DNS, discovery that occurs on the client side, and discovery that occurs on the server side. The Domain Name System (DNS) is used in DNS-based discovery, which is the process of mapping a domain name to an IP address (DNS). In client-side discovery, the client application communicates with a service registry to determine the location of the requested service. On the other hand, in server-side discovery, the server application communicates with a service registry to register itself and advertise its availability.

In containerized environments, where applications are frequently dispersed across numerous containers that are executing on separate hosts, service discovery is of special significance. Platforms for container orchestration such as Kubernetes and Docker Swarm, among others, are equipped with built-in service discovery capabilities that can be used to manage containerized services.

Automating the process of service discovery and making it easier for administrators to handle large-scale distributed systems is one of the many benefits that can be gained from using network automation. It is possible to utilise automation tools to automatically detect new services as they are being deployed and then update the service register accordingly. This helps to guarantee that all of the services within the system are registered in the correct manner and are accessible to the other services.

In addition, network automation can help to improve the system's performance and reliability by automatically monitoring and controlling the network infrastructure. This is accomplished through the use of the network. This can include load balancing and automated failover, both of which can be utilised to ensure that services are always available and responsive to users' needs. Moreover, network automation can assist in the detection and resolution of problems before they escalate to a critical state, hence lowering the amount of time the network is offline and increasing the overall quality of service.

To summarize, service discovery is an essential part of modern networking because it enables administrators to more efficiently manage large-scale distributed systems.

Automating Service Discovery with Zookeeper

Understanding Service Discovery

The process of automatically discovering and registering new services when they are added to or withdrawn from a network is what is meant by the term "automating service discovery." This is significant because it enables professionals in the networking industry to manage and monitor their networks in an effective manner, which in turn ensures that services are always available to users and can be accessed by them.

Zookeeper is a distributed coordination service that allows apps to register themselves and offers a means for other applications to discover them. It is a popular tool for automating the process of service discovery, and it is one of the most common tools used. The Go Zookeeper client library and the Go service discovery framework are two examples of the many tools and libraries that are available in Go that may be used to automate the process of discovering available services.

Practical Demonstration to Automate Service Discovery

To illustrate how to automate service discovery using Go and Zookeeper, we can build a straightforward web application that first registers itself with Zookeeper and then responds to queries from customers. This will allow us to demonstrate how to automate service discovery.

Here are the steps to do this:

Install and configure Zookeeper

First, we need to install and configure Zookeeper on a server or cluster of servers. This involves downloading the Zookeeper binary, configuring the Zookeeper configuration file, and starting the Zookeeper server.

Install the Go Zookeeper client library

Next, we need to install the Go Zookeeper client library, which provides a simple API for interacting with Zookeeper from Go. We can use the following command to install the library:

go get github.com/samuel/go-zookeeper/zk

Create a Go application

Now we can create a Go application that registers itself with Zookeeper and serves requests from clients. The application should use the Go Zookeeper client library to connect to Zookeeper and register itself as a service. Below is an example code snippet:

```
package main

import (
        "fmt"
        "net/http"
        "os"

        "github.com/samuel/go-zookeeper/zk"
```

```go
)

func main() {
        // Connect to Zookeeper
        zkConn, _, err := zk.Connect([]string{"localhost"}, time.Second)
        if err != nil {
                fmt.Println(err)
                os.Exit(1)
        }

        // Register the service
        servicePath := "/services/my-web-app"
        serviceData := []byte("http://localhost:8080")
        _, err = zkConn.Create(servicePath, serviceData, zk.FlagEphemeral,
zk.WorldACL(zk.PermAll))
        if err != nil {
                fmt.Println(err)
                os.Exit(1)
        }

        // Serve requests
        http.HandleFunc("/", func(w http.ResponseWriter, r *http.Request) {
                fmt.Fprintln(w, "Hello, world!")
        })
        http.ListenAndServe(":8080", nil)
}
```

This code registers a service with Zookeeper at the path "/services/my-web-app" and serves HTTP requests on port 8080.

Run the application

Finally, we can run the application and verify that it registers itself with Zookeeper and serves requests from clients. We can use the following command to run the application:

go run main.go

This will start the web server and register the service with Zookeeper. We can then use a Zookeeper client to verify that the service has been registered correctly.

To summarize, automating service discovery is an important part of managing modern networks and applications. By using tools like Go and Zookeeper, networking professionals can automate the process of identifying and registering new services, which helps to ensure that their networks are always efficient and responsive to user needs.

Essentials of Load Balancers

In today's modern networking design, load balancers are an essential component that disperse incoming network traffic among various servers or resources. A load balancer's principal function is to improve the availability, scalability, and dependability of the network services and applications it manages.

Load balancers are required because modern applications are frequently deployed on numerous servers or resources, and these servers or resources are able to more effectively manage incoming traffic when the load is distributed evenly among all of them. Load balancers are devices that help prevent network services and applications from becoming overloaded and guarantee that they are always accessible to users and able to respond to their requests.

Load balancers have the potential to confer a number of advantages on networking, including the following:

Increased Availability Load balancers have the capacity to disperse traffic across numerous servers, which lowers the likelihood of downtime occurring as a result of a malfunctioning piece of hardware, a clogged network, or a crashing application. Load balancers have the ability to identify faults in individual servers and then reroute traffic to other servers where it may be processed, ensuring that the service or application in question is always accessible.

Scalability: Load balancers have the ability to handle spikes in traffic by immediately rerouting it to the available servers. This helps to avoid servers from becoming overloaded and ensures that application performance remains at its peak.

Load balancers have the ability to ensure that incoming traffic is routed to the server that is closest to the user or the one that is most responsive to requests. This helps to reduce latency and enhances the overall user experience.

Reduced Admin Overhead Load balancers may manage and configure servers through a single interface, which significantly minimises the amount of administrative work that needs to be done and simplifies network management.

There are a variety of methods that can be used to create load balancers, such as DNS-based load balancing, software-based load balancing, and hardware-based load balancing. In addition, there are a variety of load balancing techniques that may be used to divide the traffic across the servers. Some examples of these algorithms include Round-Robin, Least Connections, IP Hash, and Weighted Round-Robin.

Load balancers, in general, are an essential component of the current networking infrastructure, and they offer a number of benefits that have the potential to enhance the scalability of applications, the user experience, and the availability of those applications.

Add or Remove Servers using Traefik

We are going to walk you through the process of writing an automation script using Go and Traefik that will automatically add or remove servers from a load balancer.

Understanding Traefik

Traefik is a popular open-source load balancer that can automatically discover new services, route traffic, and perform health checks. Traefik is also highly extensible and can be configured using the API. We can use the Traefik API and the Go programming language to automate the process of adding or removing servers from a load balancer.

Procedure to Add/Remove Servers from Load Balancers

Here are the steps to write an automation script to automatically add or remove servers from a load balancer using Go and Traefik:

Install Traefik and start the Traefik server
We can install Traefik on our server using the package manager or by downloading the binary. After installing Traefik, we need to start the Traefik server.

Configure Traefik to use the API
To use the Traefik API, we need to enable the API in the Traefik configuration file. We can add the following configuration to the Traefik configuration file:

```
[api]
  dashboard = true
  debug = true
```

Write the Go program

We can use the Go programming language to interact with the Traefik API. Below is an example program that adds and removes servers from a load balancer:

```go
package main

import (
    "encoding/json"
    "fmt"
    "net/http"
    "strings"
)

func main() {
    // The URL of the Traefik API
    url := "http://localhost:8080/api/providers/docker/frontends/frontend/servers"

    // The IP address of the server to add or remove
    ip := "10.0.0.1"

    // Check if the server is already in the load balancer
    inLoadBalancer := checkIfInLoadBalancer(ip, url)

    // If the server is not in the load balancer, add it
    if !inLoadBalancer {
        addServer(ip, url)
    }

    // If the server is in the load balancer, remove it
    if inLoadBalancer {
        removeServer(ip, url)
    }
}

// Check if a server is already in the load balancer
func checkIfInLoadBalancer(ip string, url string) bool {
    resp, err := http.Get(url)
```

```go
    if err != nil {
        fmt.Println("Error:", err)
    }
    defer resp.Body.Close()

    var servers []map[string]interface{}
    json.NewDecoder(resp.Body).Decode(&servers)

    for _, server := range servers {
        serverURL := server["url"].(string)
        if strings.Contains(serverURL, ip) {
            return true
        }
    }

    return false
}

// Add a server to the load balancer
func addServer(ip string, url string) {
    req, err := http.NewRequest("POST", url, nil)
    if err != nil {
        fmt.Println("Error:", err)
    }
    req.Header.Set("Content-Type", "application/json")

    server := make(map[string]string)
    server["url"] = "http://" + ip
    data, err := json.Marshal(server)
    if err != nil {
        fmt.Println("Error:", err)
    }

    client := &http.Client{}
    _, err = client.Do(req)
    if err != nil {
        fmt.Println("Error:", err)
```

```
    }
}

// Remove a server from the load balancer
func removeServer(ip string, url string) {
    resp, err := http.Get(url)
    if err != nil {
        fmt.Println("Error:", err)
    }
    defer resp.Body.Close()
}
```

Configure Load Balancing Algorithms

Below is an example of how to configure load balancing algorithms using Go and the Go reverse proxy library:

```
package main

import (
    "fmt"
    "log"
    "net/http"
    "net/http/httputil"
    "net/url"
)

func main() {
    // Define the upstream servers
    server1 := "http://localhost:8000"
    server2 := "http://localhost:8001"

    // Parse the server URLs
    url1, err := url.Parse(server1)
    if err != nil {
        log.Fatal(err)
    }
```

```go
    url2, err := url.Parse(server2)
    if err != nil {
        log.Fatal(err)
    }


    // Define the reverse proxy
    proxy := httputil.NewSingleHostReverseProxy(url1)

    // Configure the load balancing algorithm
    director := proxy.Director
    proxy.Director = func(req *http.Request) {
        // Switch to server2 if server1 fails
        if req.URL.Host == url1.Host && req.URL.Path == "/health-check" {
            req.URL.Host = url2.Host
        }
        director(req)
    }

    // Start the HTTP server
    http.HandleFunc("/", func(w http.ResponseWriter, req *http.Request) {
        proxy.ServeHTTP(w, req)
    })
    fmt.Println("Starting server on port 8080")
    log.Fatal(http.ListenAndServe(":8080", nil))
}
```

In the above sample program, we define two upstream servers (server1 and server2) and parse their URLs using the url.Parse function. We then create a reverse proxy using the httputil.NewSingleHostReverseProxy function, passing in the URL of server1.

To configure the load balancing algorithm, we define a director function that takes an http.Request and modifies its URL field to switch to server2 if server1 fails. We then set the proxy.Director field to this function.

Finally, we start an HTTP server using the http.HandleFunc function and call proxy.ServeHTTP to handle incoming requests.

When the load balancing algorithm is triggered (in this case, by requesting the /health-check path), the director function switches to server2, ensuring that requests are evenly distributed between the two upstream servers.

Note that this example uses a simple algorithm that switches to server2 if server1 fails. You may want to use a more sophisticated algorithm, such as round-robin or weighted round-robin, to ensure that the workload is evenly distributed between the upstream servers.

Summary

In this chapter, we discussed container scheduling techniques, service discovery, load balancing, and how to automate these processes using Go.

We started by explaining the different container scheduling techniques, including round-robin, least connection, IP Hash, and random. These techniques distribute traffic across multiple servers and ensure that the load is balanced, reducing the chances of a single server becoming overloaded.

Next, we discussed the importance of service discovery, which allows containers to communicate with each other without needing to know each other's IP addresses. We looked at how Zookeeper can be used to automate service discovery and demonstrated a sample use-case of automating service discovery with Go and Zookeeper.

We then moved on to load balancing and how it benefits networking. We explained that load balancing distributes traffic across multiple servers, ensuring that the load is evenly distributed, and no server becomes overloaded. We also discussed how load balancing algorithms such as round-robin, least connection, and IP Hash can be used to determine which server should receive the traffic.

We then demonstrated how to automate the process of adding or removing servers from a load balancer using Go and Traefik. We also explained how to configure load balancing algorithms practically in Go.

Next, we discussed the importance of container-native storage and how it can be managed using Go libraries. We looked at how monitoring container performance is crucial for identifying performance bottlenecks and ensuring that containers are running smoothly. Finally, we discussed the importance of rolling updates and demonstrated how to automate rolling updates using Go. We also explained how to automate firewall configuration and Kubernetes network policies using Go.

In summary, this chapter provided a comprehensive overview of container scheduling, service discovery, load balancing, container-native storage, monitoring container performance, rolling updates, firewall configuration, and Kubernetes network policies. We demonstrated practical examples of how to automate these processes using Go and Go libraries, providing a useful resource for networking professionals looking to improve their container orchestration skills.

CHAPTER 8: AUTOMATE SSL, CONTAINER-NATIVE STORAGE AND PERFORMANCE

SSL Security Protocol

SSL certificates are an essential component of secure network communications. SSL stands for Secure Sockets Layer, which is a protocol for establishing secure connections between a client and server. SSL certificates are digital certificates that provide authentication and encryption for data transferred between two parties. They help protect sensitive information such as usernames, passwords, and credit card numbers from being intercepted by unauthorized parties.

One of the primary advantages of SSL certificates is the encryption of data. SSL certificates use a process called public key encryption to protect data in transit. When a client and server establish an SSL connection, they exchange public keys that are used to encrypt and decrypt data. This means that even if an attacker intercepts the data being transmitted, they will not be able to read it because it is encrypted.

SSL certificates also provide authentication. Before an SSL connection can be established, the server must present a valid SSL certificate that is issued by a trusted Certificate Authority (CA). The SSL certificate contains information about the identity of the website owner, such as the domain name and organization name. This ensures that the client is communicating with the correct website and not an imposter.

Another advantage of SSL certificates is that they improve website rankings in search engines. Google and other search engines prioritize websites that use SSL certificates because they are considered more secure. Websites that use SSL certificates are also indicated by a padlock icon in the browser address bar, which provides users with a visual cue that the website is secure.

SSL certificates can also help prevent phishing attacks. Phishing attacks are a type of social engineering attack in which an attacker sends a fraudulent email or website that impersonates a legitimate website. The attacker may use a domain name that is similar to the legitimate website in an attempt to trick users into entering their login credentials. SSL certificates help prevent this type of attack by verifying the identity of the website owner.

In summary, SSL certificates provide encryption, authentication, and help prevent phishing attacks. They are essential for secure network communications and can help improve website rankings in search engines.

Automate Setting Up SSL Certificates

Below is a practical demonstration of automating the setup of SSL certificates using Go:

Install and Import Necessary Libraries

First, we need to install and import the necessary Go libraries. In this case, we'll use the "crypto/tls" and "net/http" packages:

```
package main

import (
        "crypto/tls"
        "net/http"
)
```

Create New HTTPS Server

Next, we'll create a new HTTPS server with a custom configuration that specifies the SSL certificate and key files:

```
func main() {
        server := &http.Server{
                Addr: ":8443",
                TLSConfig: &tls.Config{
                        Certificates: []tls.Certificate{loadCertificate()},
                },
        }

        http.HandleFunc("/", func(w http.ResponseWriter, r *http.Request) {
                w.Write([]byte("Hello, World!"))
        })

        server.ListenAndServeTLS("", "")
}
```

The loadCertificate() function loads the SSL certificate and key files from disk and returns a tls.Certificate object. In the above sample program, we assume the files are located in the current directory and named server.crt and server.key.

Generate Self-signed SSL Certificate

Before we can run the HTTPS server, we need to generate a self-signed SSL certificate. We can use the "crypto/tls" package to do this:

```go
func loadCertificate() tls.Certificate {
        cert, err := tls.LoadX509KeyPair("server.crt", "server.key")
        if err != nil {
                // If the certificate files don't exist, generate a new self-signed
certificate
                cert, err = generateCertificate()
                if err != nil {
                        panic(err)
                }
        }
        return cert
}

func generateCertificate() (tls.Certificate, error) {
        // Generate a new self-signed certificate
        template := x509.Certificate{
                SerialNumber: big.NewInt(1),
                Subject: pkix.Name{
                        CommonName: "localhost",
                },
                NotBefore: time.Now(),
                NotAfter:  time.Now().Add(365 * 24 * time.Hour),
                KeyUsage:            x509.KeyUsageKeyEncipherment      |
x509.KeyUsageDigitalSignature,
                ExtKeyUsage: []x509.ExtKeyUsage{
                        x509.ExtKeyUsageServerAuth,
                },
        }

        priv, err := rsa.GenerateKey(rand.Reader, 2048)
        if err != nil {
                return tls.Certificate{}, err
        }

        derBytes, err := x509.CreateCertificate(rand.Reader,   &template,
```

```
&template, &priv.PublicKey, priv)
     if err != nil {
          return tls.Certificate{}, err
     }

     cert := tls.Certificate{
          Certificate: [][]byte{derBytes},
          PrivateKey:  priv,
     }

     // Save the new certificate to disk
     err = ioutil.WriteFile("server.crt", cert.Certificate[0], 0644)
     if err != nil {
          return tls.Certificate{}, err
     }

     err                    =                    ioutil.WriteFile("server.key",
x509.MarshalPKCS1PrivateKey(priv), 0600)
     if err != nil {
          return tls.Certificate{}, err
     }

     return cert, nil
}
```

The loadCertificate() function first tries to load the SSL certificate and key files from disk. If they don't exist, it calls the generateCertificate() function to generate a new self-signed certificate and save it to disk.

The generateCertificate() function uses the "crypto/x509" and "math/big" packages to generate a new self-signed SSL certificate. It saves the certificate and key files

Container-native Storage

The term "container-native storage" refers to a type of storage that has been developed especially for use in environments that are containerized. It provides storage services that are designed for the dynamic and distributed nature of containerized applications, and it can be linked with container orchestration systems in a way that is completely seamless.

Conventional storage solutions were developed for physical servers, and as a result, they are not well suited for use in environments that make use of containers. They frequently fall short of the requirements for flexibility, scalability, and agility that modern containerized systems must meet. On the other hand, container-native storage solutions are created to cater to the specific needs of containerized applications with regard to storage.

Storage that is inherent to containers offers many benefits to the settings in which they are used. To begin, it is very scalable and has the capability of being quickly expanded to meet the ever-increasing demands placed on storage space. Second, it is meant to have a high availability, which ensures that data is constantly accessible and that applications can continue to run even if there is a problem with the storage. Thirdly, it has a high degree of adaptability and is simple to connect with container orchestration systems like Kubernetes. This facilitates the automated provisioning and administration of storage resources.

In addition to these advantages, container-native storage also offers a number of other capabilities that are specifically designed for use in settings that are based on containers. For instance, it offers support for snapshots and clones at the container level. These features make it possible to rapidly and effectively create new containers based on previously created ones. In addition to this, it enables thin provisioning, which is a method for making effective use of available storage space by assigning space for data only when that space is required.

In general, container-native storage is an essential element of today's modern containerized applications. It not only ensures high availability and advanced capabilities that are specifically targeted to container settings, but it also delivers the flexibility, scalability, and agility required to support these applications.

Manage Container Storage using Docker
Procedure to Work with Docker Storage

Managing container storage is an important aspect of container orchestration. With the help of Go and Go libraries, we can easily manage container storage in a distributed system. In this section, we will explore how to manage container storage using Go and Go libraries.

One of the most popular container storage solutions is Docker Storage. Docker Storage allows us to store, manage, and manipulate data for our containers. Docker Storage provides several storage drivers that can be used to store container data. Some of the most popular drivers are overlay2, aufs, and devicemapper.

To manage Docker Storage using Go, we need to use the Docker API. The Docker API allows us to interact with Docker Storage programmatically. To use the Docker API, we need to install the Docker Engine on our system. Once Docker Engine is installed, we can use the Docker CLI to interact with it.

To interact with the Docker API using Go, we can use the Docker client library. The Docker client library provides an easy-to-use interface to interact with the Docker API using Go. We can use the Docker client library to manage container storage, images, and networks.

Using Docker Client to Create New Container

Below is an example Go code that demonstrates how to use the Docker client library to create a new container with a mounted volume:

```
package main

import (
        "context"
        "fmt"
        "github.com/docker/docker/api/types"
        "github.com/docker/docker/api/types/container"
        "github.com/docker/docker/client"
        "github.com/docker/docker/pkg/stdcopy"
        "io"
        "os"
)

func main() {
        ctx := context.Background()

        cli,        err        :=        client.NewClientWithOpts(client.FromEnv,
client.WithAPIVersionNegotiation())
        if err != nil {
                panic(err)
        }

        // Pull the latest image
```

```go
out, err := cli.ImagePull(ctx, "nginx:latest", types.ImagePullOptions{})
if err != nil {
        panic(err)
}
io.Copy(os.Stdout, out)

// Create the container
resp, err := cli.ContainerCreate(ctx, &container.Config{
        Image: "nginx:latest",
}, &container.HostConfig{
        Binds: []string{"/path/on/host:/path/on/container"},
}, nil, nil, "")
if err != nil {
        panic(err)
}

// Start the container
if err := cli.ContainerStart(ctx, resp.ID, types.ContainerStartOptions{});
err != nil {
        panic(err)
}

// Attach to the container logs
out, err = cli.ContainerLogs(ctx, resp.ID,
types.ContainerLogsOptions{ShowStdout: true, Follow: true})
if err != nil {
        panic(err)
}
defer out.Close()

stdcopy.StdCopy(os.Stdout, os.Stderr, out)
}
```

In this code, we are using the Docker client library to pull the latest nginx image, create a new container with a mounted volume, and start the container. We are also using the Docker client library to attach to the container logs and print them to the console.

We can also use the Go standard library to manage container storage. The os and io packages in the Go standard library provide functions to create, read, write, and delete files and directories.

Create File inside Container

Below is an example Go code that demonstrates how to use the os and io packages to create a file inside a container:

```go
package main

import (
        "io/ioutil"
        "os"
        "path/filepath"
)

func main() {
        dir, err := ioutil.TempDir("", "example")
        if err != nil {
                panic(err)
        }
        defer os.RemoveAll(dir)

        filename := filepath.Join(dir, "example.txt")
        if err := ioutil.WriteFile(filename, []byte("Hello, World!"), 0666); err !=
nil {
                panic(err)
        }
}
```

Benefit of Container Performance

The process of developing, deploying, and managing applications has been completely transformed as a result of containerization. Containers bring with them additional problems to monitor the performance of both the containers themselves and the programmes that are operating inside of them, despite the fact that containers offer several benefits such as scalability, portability, and efficient use of resources.

It is vital to monitor the performance of containers for a few different reasons:

Containers share the resources of the host machine with the host machine, including the CPU, memory, and network bandwidth. Monitoring performance is an important part of ensuring that resources are distributed in an effective and efficient manner.

Containerization makes it possible to auto-scale resources according to the amount of work being done. While scaling up or down, it is necessary to monitor the performance of the containers to determine whether or not they are able to deal with the burden.

Containerized apps can be complicated, but performance monitoring can assist in locating performance bottlenecks and debugging any problems that may arise.

Monitoring the performance of containers can assist uncover potential security risks, such as unusual network traffic or efforts to gain unauthorised access.

Monitoring an organization's performance to ensure compliance with regulations is frequently necessary.

Monitoring the performance of containers is essential for ensuring that containerized applications function at their highest possible level, are secure, and satisfy the requirements set forth for compliance.

Monitoring the performance of containers is possible with the help of a wide variety of tools and technologies. These tools and technologies include container-native monitoring tools such as Prometheus and cAdvisor, as well as third-party monitoring tools such as Datadog and New Relic. These tools assist in monitoring performance parameters such as the utilisation of CPU and memory, as well as application response times and network traffic. Administrators are able to spot performance issues and make informed decisions regarding resource allocation and scaling by monitoring these data.

Using Go to Monitor Container Performance

The given below is a brief explanation and a practical demonstration of how to monitor container performance using Go codes:

Monitoring container performance is essential to ensure that they are running optimally and to identify any issues that may arise. There are several metrics that can be monitored, such as CPU usage, memory usage, network traffic, and disk usage.

To monitor container performance using Go, we can make use of the Docker API, which provides access to various performance metrics for containers. The Docker API can be accessed using the Docker client library for Go, which provides a simple interface for interacting with Docker.

The given below is an example Go code that demonstrates how to monitor the CPU usage of a container:

```go
package main

import (
    "context"
    "fmt"

    "github.com/docker/docker/api/types"
    "github.com/docker/docker/client"
)

func main() {
    // Create a new Docker client
    cli, err := client.NewClientWithOpts(client.FromEnv, client.WithAPIVersionNegotiation())
    if err != nil {
        panic(err)
    }

    // Get the container ID
    containerID := "your-container-id"

    // Create a context
    ctx := context.Background()

    // Get the container stats
    stats, err := cli.ContainerStats(ctx, containerID, false)
    if err != nil {
        panic(err)
    }
    defer stats.Body.Close()

    // Read the container stats
```

```go
var statsJSON types.StatsJSON
if err := json.NewDecoder(stats.Body).Decode(&statsJSON); err != nil {
    panic(err)
}

// Print the CPU usage percentage
cpuPercent := calculateCPUPercentUnix(statsJSON)
fmt.Printf("Container CPU Usage: %0.2f%%\n", cpuPercent)
}

// Calculate the CPU usage percentage
func calculateCPUPercentUnix(stats types.StatsJSON) float64 {
    cpuPercent := 0.0

    cpuDelta := float64(stats.CPUStats.CPUUsage.TotalUsage) - float64(stats.PreCPUStats.CPUUsage.TotalUsage)
    systemDelta := float64(stats.CPUStats.SystemUsage) - float64(stats.PreCPUStats.SystemUsage)
    if systemDelta > 0.0 && cpuDelta > 0.0 {
        cpuPercent = (cpuDelta / systemDelta) * float64(len(stats.CPUStats.CPUUsage.PercpuUsage)) * 100.0
    }

    return cpuPercent
}
```

This code uses the Docker client library to connect to the Docker daemon and retrieve the stats for a container. It then calculates the CPU usage percentage based on the container stats and prints it to the console.

There are many other metrics that can be monitored, and there are various libraries and tools available to make monitoring easier, such as Prometheus and Grafana.

Automate Deployment of Updates

Rolling updates are a process of updating a system or application by gradually replacing old instances with new ones. This ensures that the system or application remains available during the update process.

To automate rolling updates using Go, we can use the Kubernetes API to manage the deployment and rollout of updated container images. Below is a sample code to demonstrate the rolling update process:

```go
package main

import (
        "context"
        "flag"
        "fmt"
        "os"

        "k8s.io/apimachinery/pkg/util/intstr"
        "k8s.io/client-go/kubernetes"
        "k8s.io/client-go/rest"
        "k8s.io/client-go/tools/clientcmd"
        appsv1 "k8s.io/api/apps/v1"
)

func main() {
        var (
                kubeconfig *string
                deployment *string
                image    *string
        )

        kubeconfig = flag.String("kubeconfig", "", "absolute path to the kubeconfig file")
        deployment = flag.String("deployment", "", "name of deployment")
        image = flag.String("image", "", "container image")

        flag.Parse()

        if *kubeconfig == "" {
                fmt.Println("Please provide a kubeconfig file path")
                os.Exit(1)
        }
```

```go
if *deployment == "" {
        fmt.Println("Please provide a deployment name")
        os.Exit(1)
}

if *image == "" {
        fmt.Println("Please provide a container image")
        os.Exit(1)
}

// Use the current context in kubeconfig
config, err := clientcmd.BuildConfigFromFlags("", *kubeconfig)
if err != nil {
        panic(err.Error())
}

// Create the clientset
clientset, err := kubernetes.NewForConfig(config)
if err != nil {
        panic(err.Error())
}

// Get the deployment
deploymentsClient := clientset.AppsV1().Deployments("")
deploymentToUpdate, err := deploymentsClient.Get(context.Background(), *deployment, metav1.GetOptions{})
if err != nil {
        panic(err)
}

// Update the deployment image
deploymentToUpdate.Spec.Template.Spec.Containers[0].Image = *image

// Update the deployment
```

```go
	_,	err	=	deploymentsClient.Update(context.Background(),
deploymentToUpdate, metav1.UpdateOptions{})
	if err != nil {
		panic(err)
	}


	// Get the rollout history
	rolloutClient := clientset.AppsV1().Rollouts("")
	rollout, err := rolloutClient.Get(context.Background(), *deployment,
metav1.GetOptions{})
	if err != nil {
		panic(err)
	}


	// Get the current replica count
	currentReplicas := rollout.Status.Replicas


	// Wait for new replica set to be created
	for {
		rollout,	err	=	rolloutClient.Get(context.Background(),
*deployment, metav1.GetOptions{})
		if err != nil {
			panic(err)
		}
		if rollout.Status.Replicas > currentReplicas {
			break
		}
		time.Sleep(5 * time.Second)
	}


	// Check the status of the rollout
	rolloutStatus := rollout.Status
	if			rolloutStatus.UpdatedReplicas		==
*deploymentToUpdate.Spec.Replicas {
		fmt.Println("Rollout successful")
	} else {
		fmt.Println("Rollout failed")
```

```
        }
}
```

This code accepts command-line arguments for the path to the Kubernetes configuration file, the name of the deployment to update, and the new container image. It uses the Kubernetes API to update the deployment with the new image, wait for the new replica set to be created, and check the status of the rollout.

To run this code, save it as a Go file, install the necessary dependencies, and run it with the appropriate command

Summary

During the chapter, we discussed various aspects of containerization and automation using Go. Some of the topics covered include:

Automating SSL: We discussed the importance of SSL certificates for secure communication between containers and how to automate the setup of SSL certificates using Go libraries like Let's Encrypt and Certbot.

Container-native storage: We explained the concept of container-native storage and how to manage container storage using Go libraries like Docker SDK.

Managing container performance: We talked about the need to monitor container performance for optimal efficiency and demonstrated how to monitor container performance using Go libraries like cAdvisor.

Automatic rolling updates: We explored the need for automatic rolling updates for containerized applications and how to automate the process using Go libraries like Kubernetes client-go.

Container scheduling techniques: We discussed the different container scheduling techniques, including round-robin, least connection, IP hash, and weighted round-robin, and demonstrated how to implement them using Go libraries like Traefik.

Automating service discovery: We talked about the importance of service discovery in networking and demonstrated how to automate service discovery using Go libraries like Zookeeper.

Load balancing algorithms: We explored the different load balancing algorithms, including round-robin, least connection, IP hash, and weighted round-robin, and demonstrated how to configure load balancing algorithms using Go libraries like Traefik.

In summary, we covered a wide range of topics related to containerization and automation using Go. By leveraging the power of Go libraries, we demonstrated how to automate various tasks, including SSL setup, container storage management, container performance monitoring, and automatic rolling updates. We also explored important networking concepts like container scheduling, service discovery, and load balancing, and demonstrated how to implement them using Go libraries like Traefik and Zookeeper. These tools and techniques are essential for building and deploying robust and scalable containerized applications.

CHAPTER 9: KUBERNETES AUTOMATION

Kubernetes Networking

Understanding Kubernetes In-Detail

Kubernetes is a widely used container orchestration technology that has fundamentally altered the manner in which programmers, system administrators, and other IT professionals deploy, manage, and scale containerized applications. Kubernetes offers a robust collection of features and capabilities that can assist in the automation of the deployment and management of applications in an environment that is dispersed. Kubernetes's capacity to reduce administrative headaches associated with maintaining containerized workloads is among the platform's most significant advantages. Kubernetes is a unified platform that can be used to manage containers, networking, storage, and security. This helps to reduce the operational duties that are associated with deploying and operating containerized applications.

Because it enables containers to connect with one another and with the outside world, networking is an essential part of the Kubernetes platform. Kubernetes offers a wide variety of networking features that, when combined, make it possible for containers to communicate with one another in a manner that is both safe and dependable. Kubernetes' networking capabilities have been built from the ground up to be extremely scalable and fault-tolerant. This ensures that applications will continue to operate normally in the event that the underlying network becomes unavailable.

The capability of Kubernetes networking to automate the configuration and management of networking resources is one of the most significant advantages offered by this component. The idea of a network fabric serves as the foundation for Kubernetes' sophisticated networking model, which is provided by the platform. A set of logical network connections can be established between the containers that comprise an application through the use of the network fabric, which is a virtual network that is produced by Kubernetes and serves as the application's backbone. Kubernetes is in charge of managing the network fabric, and it makes certain that the proper networking resources are allotted to each container in accordance with the requirements of that container.

Kubernetes's ability to support a diverse set of networking protocols and technologies is another another important advantage of the platform's networking capabilities. Kubernetes has support for a wide variety of networking technologies, such as cloud networking, virtual networks, and software-defined networks. This gives programmers and system administrators the ability to select the networking technology that is most appropriate for the application and the infrastructure they are working with.

Kubernetes also offers a robust collection of networking features that, when combined, make it possible for containers to communicate with one another in a manner that is both safe and dependable. Load balancing, service discovery, and network policies are some of the characteristics that are included here. In order to ensure that an application can scale horizontally to meet changing demands, load balancing is used to spread traffic across many instances of the programme. Service discovery is what makes it possible for containers to easily connect with one another within a Kubernetes cluster. It is used to automatically discover the location of services that are contained within the cluster. The implementation of network policies allows for the restriction of access to network resources. This helps to ensure that sensitive data is kept private and that containers are able to communicate with one another in a risk-free environment.

Because it makes it possible for containers to connect with one another and with the outside world, networking is an essential component to the success of Kubernetes. Kubernetes offers a robust collection of networking features that, when combined, make it possible for containers to communicate with one another in a manner that is both safe and dependable. Because of the fault-tolerant and highly scalable nature of these characteristics, they make it possible for applications to continue operating normally even in the event that the underlying network is unavailable. Kubernetes also offers a unified platform for managing containers, networking, storage, and security. This feature contributes to the simplification of the operational duties that are connected with deploying and operating containerized applications.

Networking Makes Kubernetes Easy

Now that we have that out of the way, let us discuss the specific ways in which networking makes running Kubernetes operations easier. The capability of Kubernetes networking to automate the configuration and management of networking resources is one of the most significant advantages offered by this component. Kubernetes offers a wide variety of networking features that simplify the process of managing networking resources for both software developers and system administrators. These characteristics are as follows:

Network Policies

Administrators are given the ability to set rules that control the flow of traffic between pods that are contained within a Kubernetes cluster through the use of network policies. These policies can be used to segregate network traffic based on the requirements of certain applications. As a result, sensitive data can be safeguarded, and network resources can be utilised in the most effective manner possible.

Load Balancing

Because it enables administrators to spread traffic across numerous instances of an application, load balancing is an essential part of the networking infrastructure that Kubernetes provides. Kubernetes includes a load balancing mechanism that may be used to automatically distribute traffic across pods. This distribution can be based on a variety of parameters, such as round-robin, session affinity, or IP hash, and it is made possible by Kubernetes' built-in load balancing system.

Kubernetes networking also has a capability known as service discovery, which is considered to be very significant. It makes it simple for apps to learn where other services are located within the Kubernetes cluster by granting them the ability to do so.

Advantages of Kubernetes Networking

Kubernetes provides various benefits to enterprises and engineers alike, including the following examples:

Container Orchestration

Kubernetes was built with the intention of orchestrating containers, which simplifies the process of managing, scaling, and deploying containerized applications. The process of deploying, growing, and managing containerized apps is all made easier by Kubernetes's automation.

Automatic Load Balancing

Kubernetes includes built-in load balancing, which ensures that traffic is spread evenly across all containers in a pod. This feature is available for your services. This is especially crucial for apps that receive a significant volume of traffic since it ensures that your application is able to handle rising traffic loads without experiencing any downtime or delays in service.

Scalability

It is a feature of Kubernetes that allows you to adjust the size of your application cluster in response to changes in demand. Because Kubernetes enables you to simply adjust the number of replicas of your application, it is much simpler to manage your resources and respond to unexpected spikes in traffic.

Fault Tolerance

Because Kubernetes was built from the ground up to be fault tolerant, it is able to automatically detect and recover from any problems that may occur. Because of this, even if some of the nodes in your cluster become inoperable, your applications will continue to function normally and without interruption.

Portability

Kubernetes was developed with the goal of allowing users to deploy it on a variety of cloud providers and infrastructure platforms. Because of this, you won't have to worry about compatibility problems or being locked in by a particular vendor when you deploy your applications on any platform.

Service Discovery and Domain Name System

Kubernetes is equipped with its own built-in service discovery and DNS, which makes it much simpler to locate and communicate with your various services.

Extensibility

Kubernetes offers a comprehensive collection of application programming interfaces (APIs) and extensions, which enables users to tailor and expand the capabilities of the platform. This enables the addition of new features and capabilities to your cluster, as well as the integration of Kubernetes with a variety of additional tools and services.

Inside Kubernetes Networking

Containers are able to communicate with one another as well as with third-party services because to Kubernetes' robust networking paradigm, which is provided by the platform. Because Kubernetes employs a flat network paradigm, each container contained within a pod is provided with its own unique IP address. Because of this, it is possible for containers to communicate with one another directly, eliminating the requirement for NAT or port forwarding.

Kubernetes also includes built-in load balancing and service discovery, which makes it simple to manage your services and distribute traffic across your containers. In Kubernetes, a logical collection of pods that function together is denoted by a concept that is referred to as "services." Because each service has its own IP address and DNS name, it is possible for several containers and services to connect with one another using these identifiers.

Moreover, Kubernetes supports a number of networking plugins, which enable you to personalise your network configuration and integrate with a variety of networking options. Weave, Flannel, and Calico are just some of the well-known plugins available.

Role of Go Networking Inside Kubernetes

Go is the programming language that was utilised to construct Kubernetes, and it also plays an important part in Kubernetes's networking capabilities. Go comes with a comprehensive collection of networking packages and tools, which makes it simple to create applications and services that run over a network.

Go Tools for Kubernetes Networking

net
This package provides a set of low-level networking primitives, such as TCP and UDP sockets, that can be used to build network applications.

net/http
This package provides a set of high-level networking primitives, such as HTTP servers and clients, that can be used to build web applications.

gRPC
This is a high-performance, open-source RPC framework that allows you to build distributed applications.

Gorilla/websocket
This is a popular package for building real-time web applications using WebSockets.

libp2p
This is a peer-to-peer networking library that provides a secure and decentralized networking infrastructure.

These libraries and tools make it easy to build scalable, high-performance network applications and services in Go, which is essential for building and operating Kubernetes clusters.

In summary, Kubernetes is a powerful container orchestration platform that offers many benefits to developers and organizations, including container orchestration, load balancing, scalability, fault tolerance, portability, service discovery

Setup K8s Cluster with kubeadm

The following are the steps to set up a Kubernetes cluster in Go with kubeadm:

First, you need to ensure that you have a running Go environment on your machine. You can download and install Go from the official website https://golang.org/dl/.

Once Go is installed, you need to download and install kubeadm. You can download the

latest version of kubeadm from the official Kubernetes website
https://kubernetes.io/docs/setup/production-environment/tools/kubeadm/install-kubeadm/.

Once kubeadm is installed, you can use it to initialize a new Kubernetes cluster. The following command initializes a new cluster with a control plane node:

sudo kubeadm init --pod-network-cidr=192.168.0.0/16

This command will output a command that you can use to join worker nodes to the cluster. Make sure to save this command for later use.

Next, you need to configure kubectl, the command-line tool used to manage Kubernetes clusters. You can do this by running the following commands:

mkdir -p $HOME/.kube
sudo cp -i /etc/kubernetes/admin.conf $HOME/.kube/config
sudo chown $(id -u):$(id -g) $HOME/.kube/config

After configuring kubectl, you need to install a pod network add-on to enable networking between pods in the cluster. You can use the following command to install the Calico network add-on:

kubectl apply -f https://docs.projectcalico.org/v3.14/manifests/calico.yaml

Finally, you can join worker nodes to the cluster by running the command that was outputted in step 3 on each worker node.

sudo kubeadm join <control-plane-host>:<control-plane-port> --token <token> --discovery-token-ca-cert-hash sha256:<hash>

After completing these steps, you will have a fully functional Kubernetes cluster up and running. You can use kubectl to manage the cluster and deploy workloads to it.

In addition to setting up a Kubernetes cluster, you can also use Go to automate common operations such as deploying applications, scaling resources, and updating configurations. With the power of Go libraries and tools, you can easily create custom controllers and operators to manage your Kubernetes workloads.

Sample Program to Setup Kubernetes Cluster

To set up a Kubernetes cluster using Go commands, we can use the "os/exec" package to run the necessary kubeadm commands in the terminal. Below is an example of a Go program that sets up a Kubernetes cluster using kubeadm:

```go
package main

import (
    "fmt"
    "os/exec"
)

func main() {
    // initialize the Kubernetes cluster with kubeadm
    initCmd := exec.Command("sudo", "kubeadm", "init")
    initOutput, err := initCmd.Output()
    if err != nil {
        panic(err)
    }
    fmt.Println(string(initOutput))

    // configure kubectl to connect to the Kubernetes API server
    configCmd := exec.Command("sudo", "cp", "/etc/kubernetes/admin.conf", "$HOME/")
    configOutput, err := configCmd.Output()
    if err != nil {
        panic(err)
    }
    fmt.Println(string(configOutput))

    // apply a network plugin for the cluster
    netCmd := exec.Command("kubectl", "apply", "-f", "https://docs.projectcalico.org/v3.19/manifests/calico.yaml")
    netOutput, err := netCmd.Output()
    if err != nil {
        panic(err)
```

```
    }
    fmt.Println(string(netOutput))
}
```

In this program, we first run the kubeadm init command using os/exec to initialize the Kubernetes cluster. We then run the sudo cp /etc/kubernetes/admin.conf $HOME/ command to copy the Kubernetes configuration file to the home directory. Finally, we run the kubectl apply -f https://docs.projectcalico.org/v3.19/manifests/calico.yaml command to apply the Calico network plugin for the cluster.

Note that this program assumes that the necessary dependencies (such as kubeadm and kubectl) have already been installed on the system. Additionally, the sudo command is used to run the kubeadm commands as a privileged user, so the user running the program will need to have sudo privileges.

Once the program is run, it will output the results of each command to the console. This can be useful for verifying that each command executed successfully and for troubleshooting any errors that may occur.

Overall, using Go to automate the setup of a Kubernetes cluster can help simplify the process and make it easier to manage. By automating the setup process, networking professionals can spend less time manually configuring the cluster and more time focusing on optimizing its performance and functionality.

Envoy Ingress Controllers
Introducing Envoy

Envoy is a high-performance, open-source proxy server designed for cloud-native applications. It is commonly used as an edge proxy and load balancer in modern application architectures. Envoy can be used as an ingress controller for Kubernetes clusters, providing a way to route incoming traffic to the appropriate services within the cluster.

An ingress controller is a Kubernetes resource that provides an entry point to the cluster for incoming traffic. It typically consists of a load balancer, a set of routing rules, and a set of backends. The load balancer distributes incoming traffic to the appropriate backend services based on the routing rules.

Envoy ingress controllers are popular because they are highly configurable and can handle a wide variety of traffic patterns. They are also designed to be highly scalable and can handle a large number of connections and requests.

Benefits of Envoy

When Envoy is used as an ingress controller in Kubernetes, it provides a number of benefits:

Flexible routing

Envoy supports a wide variety of routing rules, allowing traffic to be directed to the appropriate backend services based on the path, host, headers, and other criteria.

Security

Envoy supports SSL/TLS encryption and can be configured to enforce security policies, such as requiring client certificates.

Scalability

Envoy is designed to be highly scalable and can handle a large number of connections and requests.

Observability

Envoy provides detailed metrics and logging information, making it easy to monitor the ingress traffic and troubleshoot issues.

Extensibility

Envoy is highly extensible and can be customized with filters and plugins to support additional functionality.

Overall, Envoy ingress controllers provide a powerful and flexible way to manage incoming traffic to Kubernetes clusters. They are highly configurable, scalable, and secure, and provide detailed observability into the ingress traffic.

Deploy Envoy Ingress Controllers using Go

Detailed Steps of Envoy Deployment

To deploy Envoy ingress controllers using Go, we can use the Kubernetes Go client library to interact with the Kubernetes API server and create the necessary Kubernetes resources for Envoy ingress.

Here are the steps to deploy Envoy ingress controllers using Go:
- Set up a Kubernetes cluster using a tool like Minikube or a cloud provider like GKE.

- Create a new Go project and add the Kubernetes Go client library as a dependency.
- Create a Kubernetes deployment for the Envoy ingress controller by creating a Deployment object in Go code.

Sample Program to Deploy Envoy

The given below is an example code snippet:

```
package main

import (
    "context"
    "fmt"

    metav1 "k8s.io/apimachinery/pkg/apis/meta/v1"
    "k8s.io/client-go/kubernetes"
    "k8s.io/client-go/rest"
)

func main() {
    // Load Kubernetes configuration from default location
    config, err := rest.InClusterConfig()
    if err != nil {
        panic(err.Error())
    }

    // Create Kubernetes clientset
    clientset, err := kubernetes.NewForConfig(config)
    if err != nil {
        panic(err.Error())
    }

    // Create Deployment object
    deployment := &appsv1.Deployment{
        ObjectMeta: metav1.ObjectMeta{
            Name: "envoy-ingress",
        },
        Spec: appsv1.DeploymentSpec{
```

```go
Replicas: int32Ptr(1),
Selector: &metav1.LabelSelector{
  MatchLabels: map[string]string{
    "app": "envoy-ingress",
  },
},
Template: corev1.PodTemplateSpec{
  ObjectMeta: metav1.ObjectMeta{
    Labels: map[string]string{
      "app": "envoy-ingress",
    },
  },
  Spec: corev1.PodSpec{
    Containers: []corev1.Container{
      {
        Name:  "envoy",
        Image: "envoyproxy/envoy:v1.19.0",
        Args: []string{
          "-c",
          "/etc/envoy-config/envoy.yaml",
        },
        VolumeMounts: []corev1.VolumeMount{
          {
            Name:      "envoy-config",
            MountPath: "/etc/envoy-config",
          },
        },
      },
    },
    Volumes: []corev1.Volume{
      {
        Name: "envoy-config",
        VolumeSource: corev1.VolumeSource{
          ConfigMap: &corev1.ConfigMapVolumeSource{
            LocalObjectReference: corev1.LocalObjectReference{
              Name: "envoy-config",
            },
```

```
                    },
                },
            },
        },
    },
},
}

    // Create Deployment in Kubernetes
    _,                                    err                         =
clientset.AppsV1().Deployments("default").Create(context.Background(),
deployment, metav1.CreateOptions{})
    if err != nil {
        panic(err.Error())
    }

    fmt.Println("Deployment created successfully")
}

func int32Ptr(i int32) *int32 { return &i }
```

This code creates a Deployment object for the Envoy ingress controller with a single replica. The Envoy container is configured with a volume mount for a ConfigMap containing the Envoy configuration file.

Install the Required Dependencies

Before deploying Envoy ingress controllers, we need to install some dependencies. We need to install Go, the Kubernetes command-line tool (kubectl), and the Helm package manager. Here are the commands to install these dependencies on a Linux machine:

```
# Install Go
sudo apt-get update
sudo apt-get install -y golang-go

# Install kubectl
sudo apt-get update && sudo apt-get install -y apt-transport-https gnupg2 curl
```

```
curl -s https://packages.cloud.google.com/apt/doc/apt-key.gpg | sudo apt-key add
-
echo "deb https://apt.kubernetes.io/ kubernetes-xenial main" | sudo tee -a
/etc/apt/sources.list.d/kubernetes.list
sudo apt-get update
sudo apt-get install -y kubectl

# Install Helm
curl https://raw.githubusercontent.com/helm/helm/main/scripts/get-helm-3   |
bash
```
Create a Kubernetes cluster:

Next, we need to create a Kubernetes cluster. We can use a tool called kubeadm to create a cluster with one master node and two worker nodes. Here are the commands to create the cluster:

```
# Initialize the cluster on the master node
sudo kubeadm init --pod-network-cidr=10.244.0.0/16

# Copy the kubeconfig file to the user's home directory
mkdir -p $HOME/.kube
sudo cp -i /etc/kubernetes/admin.conf $HOME/.kube/config
sudo chown $(id -u):$(id -g) $HOME/.kube/config

# Install the Flannel network add-on
kubectl                          apply                              -f
https://raw.githubusercontent.com/coreos/flannel/master/Documentation/kube-
flannel.yml
```

This will create a Kubernetes cluster with one master node and two worker nodes. The Flannel network add-on will be used to provide networking between the pods in the cluster.

Deploy Envoy Ingress Controller using Helm

Once the Kubernetes cluster is up and running, we can deploy the Envoy ingress controller using Helm. Helm is a package manager for Kubernetes that allows us to easily deploy applications and services to a cluster.

Here are the commands to deploy the Envoy ingress controller using Helm:

```
# Add the Helm repository for the Envoy ingress controller
helm repo add envoy https://helm.github.io/charts

# Update the local Helm chart repository
helm repo update

# Install the Envoy ingress controller
helm install envoy envoy/envoy
```

This will deploy the Envoy ingress controller to the Kubernetes cluster. The ingress controller will be configured to use the Flannel network add-on for networking.

Create an Ingress Resource

Finally, we need to create an Ingress resource to route traffic to our application. An Ingress resource is a Kubernetes object that defines rules for routing external traffic to internal services.

Below is an example Ingress resource that routes traffic to a service named my-service:

```
apiVersion: networking.k8s.io/v1
kind: Ingress
metadata:
  name: my-ingress
  annotations:
    kubernetes.io/ingress.class: "envoy"
spec:
  rules:
  - http:
      paths:
      - path: /my-path
        pathType: Prefix
        backend:
          service:
            name: my-service
            port:
```

```
     name: http
```

Once the deployment is created, we can expose the envoy service by creating a Kubernetes service object.

The given below is an example of creating a service object for the envoy deployment:

```
apiVersion: v1
kind: Service
metadata:
  name: envoy
spec:
  type: NodePort
  selector:
    app: envoy
  ports:
    - name: http
      port: 80
      targetPort: 80
      protocol: TCP
    - name: https
      port: 443
      targetPort: 443
      protocol: TCP
```

This service object will create a NodePort service for the envoy deployment, which will expose port 80 and 443 on each node in the Kubernetes cluster. We can then access the envoy ingress controller using the IP address of any node in the cluster, on the ports that we've specified.

Finally, we can configure our Kubernetes cluster to use the envoy ingress controller as the default ingress controller, by setting the ingressClass annotation in our ingress resources.

The given below is an example:

```
apiVersion: networking.k8s.io/v1
kind: Ingress
metadata:
```

```
      name: my-ingress
      annotations:
        kubernetes.io/ingress.class: "envoy"
    spec:
      rules:
      - host: example.com
        http:
          paths:
          - path: /foo
            backend:
              serviceName: foo-service
              servicePort: 80
          - path: /bar
            backend:
              serviceName: bar-service
              servicePort: 80
```

In the above sample program, we've set the kubernetes.io/ingress.class annotation to "envoy", which tells Kubernetes to use the envoy ingress controller for this ingress resource. We've also defined some routing rules for the example.com hostname.

And that's it! With these steps, we've deployed an envoy ingress controller in our Kubernetes cluster, and configured our cluster to use it as the default ingress controller. We can now use the envoy features to route traffic to our Kubernetes services based on various criteria, such as hostname, path, or header values.

Summary

In this chapter, we discussed Kubernetes networking, including the importance of networking for Kubernetes operations and the role of networking in simplifying Kubernetes operations. We also discussed how to set up a Kubernetes cluster using kubeadm, and provided a practical example of a program to set up a Kubernetes cluster using Go commands.

We then discussed Envoy ingress controllers, which provide load balancing and traffic routing capabilities for Kubernetes services. We explained the concept of ingress controllers and how Envoy works as an ingress controller, and then provided practical steps for deploying Envoy ingress controllers using Go.

Next, we discussed service mesh, which provides a way to manage communication between microservices in a Kubernetes cluster. We explained the role of service mesh in improving visibility, security, and scalability for microservices, and then provided steps for implementing service mesh with Linkerd and Go.

Finally, we discussed how to automate firewall configuration and Kubernetes network policies using Go. We provided practical steps for automating firewall configuration and Kubernetes network policies, and then provided sample Go programs that demonstrate these steps.

Overall, this chapter covered a range of important topics related to Kubernetes networking and operations, providing both conceptual explanations and practical examples to help readers understand these topics and apply them in their own projects.

CHAPTER 10: SERVICE MESH, FIREWALL AND NETWORK POLICIES

Understanding Service Mesh

Overview

Service mesh is a term that refers to the management of service-to-service communication within a microservices-based application. It is essentially an infrastructure layer that manages communication between microservices, including request routing, traffic management, service discovery, security, and observability. A service mesh typically consists of a set of network proxies (or sidecars) deployed alongside each microservice in the application.

Service mesh emerged as a response to the increasing complexity of microservices-based applications. As these applications grew in size and number of services, it became increasingly difficult to manage service-to-service communication. Traditional approaches, such as manual configuration of network devices and load balancers, became untenable in such environments. Service mesh provides a solution to these challenges by decoupling the network from the application code and providing a dedicated layer of infrastructure to manage service-to-service communication.

Advantages of Service Mesh

One of the key benefits of service mesh is that it provides a uniform method for managing communication across multiple languages and frameworks. In a microservices architecture, services may be written in different programming languages and use different frameworks. Service mesh abstracts away these differences, providing a consistent set of APIs for communication between services. This allows developers to focus on application code, rather than the complexities of networking.

Another benefit of service mesh is that it provides a rich set of features for managing service-to-service communication. For example, service mesh can provide advanced traffic management capabilities, such as load balancing, circuit breaking, and retry logic. It can also handle service discovery, allowing services to dynamically discover and communicate with other services. In addition, service mesh can provide security features, such as mutual TLS authentication, encryption, and access control. Finally, service mesh provides observability into the network, allowing operators to monitor and troubleshoot application traffic in real-time.

Service mesh is typically implemented using a set of network proxies or sidecars deployed alongside each microservice. These proxies handle all inbound and outbound traffic for the service, providing advanced traffic management, security, and observability features. The proxies communicate with each other and with a control plane, which manages the configuration and policies for the service mesh.

Service Mesh Tools

There are several popular service mesh implementations available today. One of the most widely used is Istio, which is an open-source service mesh developed by Google, IBM, and Lyft. Istio provides advanced traffic management features, such as load balancing, traffic shaping, and fault injection, as well as security features like mutual TLS authentication and access control. Istio also provides observability features, including distributed tracing, metrics, and logs.

Another popular service mesh is Linkerd, which is an open-source service mesh developed by Buoyant. Linkerd provides similar features to Istio, including advanced traffic management, security, and observability. However, Linkerd is designed to be lightweight and easy to deploy, making it a good choice for smaller deployments.

In conclusion, service mesh provides a powerful infrastructure layer for managing service-to-service communication in microservices-based applications. It abstracts away the complexities of networking, provides a uniform method for communication across multiple languages and frameworks, and provides advanced traffic management, security, and observability features. As microservices-based applications continue to grow in complexity, service mesh is becoming an increasingly important tool for developers and operators alike.

Service Mesh with Linkerd

Procedure to Adopt Service Mesh

Implementing service mesh with Linkerd and Go involves several steps. Below is a brief overview of the process:

Install and configure Linkerd
The first step is to install and configure Linkerd. You can follow the official documentation to do this. Once you have installed Linkerd, you need to configure it to work with your Kubernetes cluster.

Deploy the application
The next step is to deploy your application to Kubernetes. You can do this using a deployment or statefulset.

Create a service

Create a service
Once your application is deployed, you need to create a Kubernetes service to expose it. This will allow Linkerd to discover and route traffic to your application.

Install Linkerd proxy
You need to install the Linkerd proxy sidecar into your application pods. This can be done automatically by adding annotations to your deployment or statefulset manifests.

Verify the setup
Once you have completed the setup, you can use the Linkerd dashboard to verify that the traffic is being routed correctly. You can also use the command-line tool to inspect the traffic and diagnose any issues.

Sample Program to Implement Linkerd Service Mesh

Below is a sample demonstration of how to implement service mesh with Linkerd and Go:

Install and Configure Linkerd

To install Linkerd, you can use the following command:

```
curl -sL https://run.linkerd.io/install | sh
```

Once Linkerd is installed, you can configure it to work with your Kubernetes cluster:

```
linkerd check --pre
linkerd install | kubectl apply -f -
linkerd check
```

Deploy the Application

To deploy the application, you can use a Kubernetes deployment manifest. Below is an example:

```
apiVersion: apps/v1
kind: Deployment
metadata:
  name: my-app
```

```
  labels:
    app: my-app
spec:
 replicas: 3
 selector:
   matchLabels:
     app: my-app
 template:
   metadata:
     labels:
       app: my-app
   spec:
     containers:
       - name: my-app
         image: my-app:v1
         ports:
           - containerPort: 8080
```

You can apply this manifest using the following command:

```
kubectl apply -f deployment.yaml
```

Create a Service

To create a Kubernetes service for your application, you can use the following manifest:

```
apiVersion: v1
kind: Service
metadata:
 name: my-app
spec:
 selector:
   app: my-app
 ports:
   - protocol: TCP
     port: 80
     targetPort: 8080
```

You can apply this manifest using the following command:

```
kubectl apply -f service.yaml
```

Install Linkerd Proxy

To install the Linkerd proxy sidecar into your application pods, you can add the following annotations to your deployment manifest:

```yaml
apiVersion: apps/v1
kind: Deployment
metadata:
  name: my-app
  labels:
    app: my-app
spec:
  replicas: 3
  selector:
    matchLabels:
      app: my-app
  template:
    metadata:
      labels:
        app: my-app
      annotations:
        linkerd.io/inject: enabled
    spec:
      containers:
        - name: my-app
          image: my-app:v1
          ports:
            - containerPort: 8080
```

You can apply this manifest using the following command:

```
kubectl apply -f deployment.yaml
```

Verify the Setup

You can use the Linkerd dashboard to verify that the traffic is being routed correctly. You can access the dashboard using the following command:

linkerd dashboard

Automate Firewall Configuration

Firewall configuration is an important aspect of network security, and automating it can help ensure consistency and reduce the risk of human error. Here are the steps to automate firewall configuration in Go:

Install the Necessary Packages

Before we can begin automating firewall configuration with Go, we need to make sure that the necessary packages are installed. On a Linux system, this can typically be done with the following command:

sudo apt-get install -y iptables-persistent

This will install the iptables-persistent package, which provides a simple way to save and restore firewall rules across reboots.

Define Firewall Rules

Once the necessary packages are installed, we can define the firewall rules that we want to automate. This can be done with the iptables command, which is used to manipulate firewall rules on Linux systems. Below is an example rule that allows incoming traffic on port 80 (HTTP):

sudo iptables -A INPUT -p tcp --dport 80 -j ACCEPT

This rule allows incoming TCP traffic on port 80 and sends it to the ACCEPT target.

Create Go Program to Automate Firewall Configuration

Now that we have defined the firewall rules that we want to automate, we can create a Go program to execute those rules. Below is an example program that automates the rule we defined above:

```go
package main

import (
    "os/exec"
)

func main() {
    cmd := exec.Command("iptables", "-A", "INPUT", "-p", "tcp", "--dport", "80",
"-j", "ACCEPT")
    err := cmd.Run()
    if err != nil {
        panic(err)
    }
}
```

This program uses the os/exec package to execute the iptables command with the necessary arguments to add the rule to the firewall.

Test the Program

Once the program is written, we can test it to ensure that it is working correctly. Simply run the program with the following command:

go run main.go

This will execute the program and add the necessary firewall rule. You can verify that the rule was added by running the iptables -L command, which will show you the current firewall rules.

Automate the Program

Finally, we can automate the program by adding it to a script or job scheduler. For example, we could create a shell script that executes the program at boot time to ensure that the firewall rules are always in place.

By following these steps, we can easily automate firewall configuration in Go, which can help ensure that our network is secure and consistent.

Sample Program to Automate Firewall

The given below is a sample program in Go that automates firewall configuration using iptables:

```go
package main

import (
        "fmt"
        "os/exec"
)

func main() {
        // Open port 80 for HTTP traffic
        cmd1 := exec.Command("iptables", "-A", "INPUT", "-p", "tcp", "--dport", "80", "-j", "ACCEPT")
        err := cmd1.Run()
        if err != nil {
                fmt.Println("Error opening port 80:", err)
                return
        }

        // Open port 443 for HTTPS traffic
        cmd2 := exec.Command("iptables", "-A", "INPUT", "-p", "tcp", "--dport", "443", "-j", "ACCEPT")
        err = cmd2.Run()
        if err != nil {
                fmt.Println("Error opening port 443:", err)
                return
        }

        // Deny all other incoming traffic
        cmd3 := exec.Command("iptables", "-A", "INPUT", "-j", "DROP")
        err = cmd3.Run()
        if err != nil {
                fmt.Println("Error blocking incoming traffic:", err)
                return
```

```
        }

        // Display the current iptables rules
        cmd4 := exec.Command("iptables", "-L")
        output, err := cmd4.Output()
        if err != nil {
                fmt.Println("Error getting iptables rules:", err)
                return
        }

        fmt.Println("Current iptables rules:\n", string(output))
}
```

This program opens port 80 for HTTP traffic, port 443 for HTTPS traffic, and blocks all other incoming traffic by default. It then displays the current iptables rules. You can modify this program to suit your specific firewall requirements.

Automate Linkerd Network Policies

To automate network policies in Linkerd, you can follow the below steps:

Install Linkerd on your Kubernetes cluster using the following command:

curl -sL run.linkerd.io/install | sh

Verify the installation by running the following command:

linkerd check --pre

Install the Linkerd control plane by running the following command:

linkerd install | kubectl apply -f -
Create a namespace in which you want to apply network policies by running the following command:

kubectl create namespace <namespace-name>

Create a Linkerd service profile for your application by running the following command:

linkerd profile --proto <path-to-protobuf-file> <service-name>.<namespace-name>.svc.cluster.local > <service-name>-profile.yaml

This command creates a service profile YAML file for your application, which you can use to define network policies.

Create a network policy YAML file that defines the allowed inbound and outbound traffic for your application. You can use the service profile YAML file created in the previous step to specify the allowed traffic.

The given below is an example network policy YAML file:

```
apiVersion: networking.k8s.io/v1
kind: NetworkPolicy
metadata:
  name: <policy-name>
  namespace: <namespace-name>
spec:
  podSelector:
    matchLabels:
      app: <app-label>
  policyTypes:
  - Ingress
  - Egress
  ingress:
  - from:
    - podSelector:
        matchLabels:
          app: <app-label>
    ports:
    - protocol: TCP
      port: <port>
  egress:
  - to:
    - podSelector:
        matchLabels:
          app: <app-label>
    ports:
```

```
  - protocol: TCP
    port: <port>
```

This network policy allows inbound and outbound traffic on a specific port for pods with a specific label.

Apply the network policy YAML file to the namespace by running the following command:

```
kubectl apply -f <policy-file>.yaml
```

This applies the network policy to the specified namespace.

By automating network policies in Linkerd, you can define granular policies to control traffic between microservices in your Kubernetes cluster. This helps to improve security and ensure that your applications are functioning as intended.

Sample Program to Automate Network Policies

Following is an example of how network policies are defined and enforced in Linkerd using Kubernetes Network Policies.

First, you need to define a network policy in Kubernetes. The given below is an example of a network policy that allows traffic only from pods labeled with app: my-app:

```
apiVersion: networking.k8s.io/v1
kind: NetworkPolicy
metadata:
  name: my-app-policy
spec:
  podSelector:
    matchLabels:
      app: my-app
  ingress:
  - from:
    - podSelector: {}
```

Next, you need to install the Linkerd CNI plugin, which will enforce the network policies in Linkerd. You can do this by running the following command:

linkerd install-cni | kubectl apply -f -

Finally, you need to enable network policy enforcement in Linkerd by adding the linkerd.io/inject: enabled label to the namespace where your pods are running. You can do this by running the following command:

kubectl annotate namespace my-namespace linkerd.io/inject=enabled

Once these steps are completed, Linkerd will automatically enforce the network policies defined in Kubernetes.

Summary

In this chapter, we discussed how to implement service mesh using Linkerd and automate firewall configurations and network policies in Kubernetes. The given below is a summary of the chapter:

We started by discussing the concept of service mesh and its benefits, including better visibility, traffic management, and security. We then talked about Linkerd, an open-source service mesh that provides a lightweight and easy-to-use solution for implementing service mesh.

Next, we discussed the steps to automate firewall configurations using Go. This included installing and configuring the firewall service, creating firewall rules, and starting and enabling the firewall service. We also talked about how to create a sample program in Go to automate these steps.

Moving on, we talked about how to implement network policies in Kubernetes using Linkerd. We discussed the concept of network policies, which are a way to control network traffic within a cluster, and how to use Linkerd to create and enforce network policies. This involved installing and configuring Linkerd, creating a network policy, and applying the policy to a namespace. We also discussed how to create a sample program in Go to automate these steps.

CHAPTER 11: NETWORK PERFORMANCE TESTING

Performance Testing

Performance testing is the process of assessing the speed, responsiveness, stability, scalability, and reliability of an application or system under various workloads and conditions. The primary objective of performance testing is to identify and mitigate any performance bottlenecks that could impact the user experience, system uptime, and business goals.

Importance of Performance Testing

Performance testing plays a crucial role in ensuring that an application or system meets the performance requirements specified by stakeholders, including customers, users, and management. Some of the key benefits of performance testing include:

Improved User Experience

By identifying and addressing performance bottlenecks, performance testing helps improve the speed, responsiveness, and stability of the system, which enhances the overall user experience.

Reduced Downtime and Maintenance Costs

Performance testing helps identify issues that could lead to downtime, which can be costly and damaging to a company's reputation. By identifying and addressing these issues proactively, performance testing can help minimize downtime and reduce maintenance costs.

Increased Scalability and Capacity

Performance testing helps assess an application's ability to handle increasing workloads and user traffic. By identifying performance bottlenecks, performance testing can help optimize the system's performance and increase its scalability and capacity.

Improved Security

Performance testing can help identify vulnerabilities and weaknesses in an application's security measures. By simulating various attack scenarios and assessing the system's response, performance testing can help identify potential security risks and help address them.

Tasks and Operations Involved in Performance Testing

Test Planning

The first step in performance testing involves defining the test objectives, test scenarios, and success criteria. This involves analyzing the system's architecture, understanding the user requirements, and defining the performance metrics to be measured.

Test Environment Setup

Performance testing requires a test environment that replicates the production environment as closely as possible. This involves configuring hardware, software, and network resources, including servers, databases, load balancers, firewalls, and other components.

Test Scripting and Execution

Test scripts are developed to simulate various user scenarios and workload patterns. These scripts are executed to generate realistic traffic and measure the system's response time, throughput, and resource utilization.

Monitoring and Analysis

Performance testing involves monitoring the system's performance metrics in real-time, including response time, resource utilization, and error rates. This data is analyzed to identify performance bottlenecks, optimize the system's performance, and generate performance reports.

Reporting and Communication

Performance testing involves documenting the test results, including performance metrics, test scripts, and analysis reports. This information is communicated to stakeholders, including developers, testers, project managers, and business leaders, to help make informed decisions about the system's performance and scalability.

Performance testing is a critical aspect of software development and infrastructure management. It helps ensure that an application or system meets performance requirements, enhances the user experience, and minimizes downtime and maintenance costs. To conduct effective performance testing, it is essential to plan the tests carefully, set up the test environment properly, develop and execute test scripts, monitor and analyze the system's performance metrics, and communicate the results effectively to stakeholders.

Automate Load Testing

Overview

Load testing is an important aspect of performance testing that helps in measuring the performance of a system under a specific load. In other words, it helps in determining how much load a system can handle before it starts to experience degradation in performance or fails completely. Load testing is particularly useful for applications that are expected to experience heavy traffic or user load.

Load testing involves simulating a high level of user traffic on a system to see how it responds. This can be done by using specialized tools that create simulated user traffic, which can be gradually increased until the system reaches its limit. The results of the load testing can be used to identify any bottlenecks or performance issues and to make adjustments to the system to optimize performance.

There are different types of load testing that can be performed, each with its own specific goals and objectives:

Volume Testing
This involves testing the system's ability to handle a large volume of data. The goal of volume testing is to determine the maximum amount of data that can be processed by the system without any issues.

Stress Testing
This type of testing is designed to measure the system's ability to handle high levels of traffic or load. The goal of stress testing is to determine the point at which the system begins to fail or degrade in performance.

Spike Testing
This involves testing the system's ability to handle sudden spikes in traffic or load. The goal of spike testing is to determine how quickly the system can respond to sudden increases in traffic and whether it can handle them without any issues.

Soak Testing
This type of testing is designed to measure the system's ability to handle a sustained load over a period of time. The goal of soak testing is to determine whether the system can maintain its performance levels over an extended period of time.

Endurance Testing
This involves testing the system's ability to handle a sustained load over a prolonged period of time. The goal of endurance testing is to determine whether the system can maintain its performance levels over an extended period of time without any issues.

The importance of load testing lies in its ability to identify performance issues and bottlenecks before they become critical problems. By identifying these issues early on, load testing allows developers and system administrators to make adjustments to the system to optimize performance, which can lead to improved user experience, increased productivity, and reduced downtime. Load testing also helps in determining the system's capacity, which is important for ensuring that the system can handle expected traffic and load.

Benefits of Load Testing

Improved system performance: By identifying performance issues early on, load testing allows developers and system administrators to make adjustments to the system to optimize performance, which can lead to improved user experience, increased productivity, and reduced downtime.

Enhanced User Experience

Load testing helps in identifying performance issues that can impact user experience, such as slow page load times, and allows for adjustments to be made to improve performance.

Increased Productivity

Load testing helps in identifying performance issues that can impact productivity, such as slow response times, and allows for adjustments to be made to improve performance.

Reduced Downtime

Load testing helps in identifying performance issues that can lead to system failures and downtime, and allows for adjustments to be made to prevent these issues from occurring.

Load testing is an important aspect of performance testing that helps in identifying performance issues and bottlenecks before they become critical problems. By identifying these issues early on, load testing allows for adjustments to be made to the system to optimize performance, which can lead to improved user experience, increased productivity, and reduced downtime.

Exploring Go Vegeta Tool

Overview

Vegeta is an open-source HTTP load testing tool written in Go. It is designed to be simple to use and highly configurable. Vegeta is widely used by developers and DevOps teams to test the performance and scalability of web applications and APIs.

The key features of Vegeta include support for HTTP/1.1 and HTTP/2, automatic rate limiting, configurable attacks and metrics, and support for custom headers and body payloads.

Installing Vegeta is a straightforward process that involves downloading the latest version of the binary file for your operating system from the official GitHub repository. Vegeta is a command-line tool, so it can be used on any system that has a terminal emulator.

Once installed, Vegeta can be used to run load tests against web applications and APIs. A typical load test using Vegeta involves specifying a target URL or set of URLs, setting the desired rate of requests per second, and configuring the attack type and duration.

Vegeta supports four types of attack patterns:
- Constant throughput: In this attack pattern, Vegeta sends a constant rate of requests per second to the target URL.
- Constant connections: In this attack pattern, Vegeta sends requests as fast as possible, maintaining a constant number of connections to the target URL.
- Spike: In this attack pattern, Vegeta starts with a low rate of requests per second and gradually increases the rate until the maximum desired rate is reached.
- Stress: In this attack pattern, Vegeta sends requests as fast as possible, with no regard for the desired rate or number of connections.

Vegeta also supports a variety of metrics, including latency distribution, success rate, and request rate. These metrics can be used to analyze the performance of the target URL under different conditions and to identify any bottlenecks or performance issues.

Benefits of Vegeta Testing Tool

Scalability
Vegeta is highly scalable and can be used to test the performance and scalability of web applications and APIs across a wide range of scenarios and load levels.

Flexibility
Vegeta is highly configurable and can be customized to meet the specific needs of different applications and use cases.

Simplicity
Vegeta is easy to use and can be integrated into existing workflows and processes with minimal effort.

Open-Source
Vegeta is open-source and free to use, which makes it accessible to developers and DevOps

teams of all sizes and budgets.

Vegeta provides a range of attack patterns and metrics that can be used to test the performance and scalability of different applications and identify any bottlenecks or performance issues. Its ease of use and scalability make it a popular choice for developers and DevOps teams looking to optimize the performance of their web applications and APIs.

Sample Program to Run Load Testing

Given below is a sample program to run load testing using Go and Vegeta:

First, make sure you have installed the Vegeta tool on your system by following the instructions provided on their official website.

Once you have installed Vegeta, you can use the following Go program to run a simple load test:

```go
package main

import (
    "fmt"
    "io/ioutil"
    "net/http"
    "time"

    "github.com/tsenart/vegeta/lib"
)

func main() {
    // Define the target URL for the load test
    target := vegeta.Target{
            Method: "GET",
            URL:    "http://example.com",
    }

    // Define the attack settings
    rate := vegeta.Rate{Freq: 100, Per: time.Second}
```

```
    duration := 5 * time.Second
    targeter := vegeta.NewStaticTargeter(target)
    attacker := vegeta.NewAttacker()

    // Run the attack and store the results
    var metrics vegeta.Metrics
    for res := range attacker.Attack(targeter, rate, duration, "Load testing
using Vegeta") {
            metrics.Add(res)
    }

    // Write the results to a file
    report := metrics.Report()
    err := ioutil.WriteFile("load_test_report.txt", []byte(report), 0644)
    if err != nil {
            fmt.Println("Error writing report to file:", err)
            return
    }

    fmt.Println("Load test completed successfully!")
}
```

In this above program, we are first importing the necessary packages - "fmt" to print output to the console, "io/ioutil" to write the load test report to a file, "net/http" to define the target URL, "time" to set the attack rate and duration, and "github.com/tsenart/vegeta/lib" to use the Vegeta tool for load testing.

Next, we define the target URL for the load test using the vegeta.Target struct, which specifies the HTTP method and URL.

We then define the attack settings, which includes the rate of requests (100 requests per second in this example), the duration of the attack (5 seconds in this example), and the targeter and attacker objects.

The targeter is responsible for generating the requests, and in this example, we are using a static targeter that will send requests to the same URL defined earlier.

The attacker object is responsible for sending the requests at the specified rate and duration, and collecting the responses.

Finally, we run the attack and store the results in the metrics object. We then write the results to a file using the ioutil.WriteFile function, and print a success message to the console.

To run this program, save it in a file named "load_test.go" and run the following command in your terminal:

```
go run load_test.go
```

This will start the load test and output a success message once it completes. You can then view the load test report in the "load_test_report.txt" file that was generated.

Stress Testing

Overview

Stress testing is a type of performance testing that is used to determine how well a system can handle a heavy load. It involves subjecting the system to a higher-than-normal load to see how it performs under pressure. Stress testing is important because it helps identify bottlenecks, performance issues, and potential failures before they become a problem in production.

Go Tools for Stress Testing

In the Go programming language, there are several tools available for stress testing. These include:

Gor

Gor is an HTTP traffic replay tool that is used for load testing, stress testing, and functional testing. It captures and replays HTTP traffic from live systems and can be used to simulate thousands of concurrent users.

Vegeta

This tool we have already introduced in previous section and known as a versatile HTTP load testing tool that allows users to attack web services with HTTP requests. It can be used to simulate a large number of users and can measure the performance of a web application under different types of loads.

Hey

Hey is an HTTP load generator, written in Go. It is used for benchmarking and testing HTTP services by generating a large number of requests.

Procedure to Run Stress Testing

To use these tools for stress testing, you need to follow the steps mentioned below:

Install Stress Testing Tool

Once you have installed Go, you can use the go get command to download and install the stress testing tool of your choice. For example, to install Vegeta, you can use the following command:

```
go get -u github.com/tsenart/vegeta
```

Create Test File

After installing the stress testing tool, you need to create a test file that specifies the load to be applied to the system. For example, to test a web server, you can create a test file in JSON format that specifies the URL to be tested, the number of requests to be made, and the rate at which the requests should be made.

Run the Test

Once you have created the test file, you can run the stress test using the stress testing tool. For example, to run a stress test using Vegeta, you can use the following command:

```
vegeta attack -targets=targets.json -rate=100 -duration=30s | vegeta report
```

This command will generate a report that shows the results of the stress test, including the number of requests made, the success rate, the response time, and the throughput.

Stress testing is an important aspect of performance testing because it helps identify performance issues and bottlenecks in a system. By simulating a heavy load, stress testing can help determine the system's capacity and identify areas that need improvement. It can also help prevent system failures and downtime by identifying potential issues before they become a problem in production.

Sample Program to Run Stress Testing

Vegeta is a powerful open-source HTTP load testing tool written in Go. It allows users to send HTTP requests at a configurable rate and collect the resulting data to generate reports. In addition to load testing, Vegeta can also be used for stress testing.

To run stress testing using Vegeta and Go, we can follow these steps:

Install Vegeta

We can install Vegeta using the following command:

```
go get -u github.com/tsenart/vegeta
```

Write a Test Script

We can write a test script in Go to define the HTTP request to be sent, the rate at which it should be sent, and the duration of the test. Here is an example script that sends a GET request to a URL with a rate of 10 requests per second for 30 seconds:

```go
package main

import (
    "fmt"
    "log"
    "os"
    "time"

    "github.com/tsenart/vegeta/lib"
)

func main() {
    rate := vegeta.Rate{Freq: 10, Per: time.Second}
    duration := 30 * time.Second
    targeter := vegeta.NewStaticTargeter(vegeta.Target{
        Method: "GET",
        URL:    "https://example.com",
    })
    attacker := vegeta.NewAttacker()

    var metrics vegeta.Metrics
    for res := range attacker.Attack(targeter, rate, duration, "Stress testing") {
```

```
        metrics.Add(res)
    }

    metrics.Close()
    fmt.Printf("99th percentile: %s\n", metrics.Latencies.P99)
    fmt.Printf("Max response time: %s\n", metrics.Latencies.Max)
    fmt.Printf("Total requests: %d\n", metrics.Requests)
    fmt.Printf("Total successes: %d\n", metrics.Successful)
    fmt.Printf("Total errors: %d\n", metrics.Errors)
}
```

In this script, we define a rate of 10 requests per second and a duration of 30 seconds. We then create a static target that sends a GET request to the URL "https://example.com". We create an attacker and use it to attack the target for the specified rate and duration. We collect the resulting metrics and print them out.

Run the Test

We can run the test script using the following command:

```
go run test.go | vegeta report
```

This command runs the test script and pipes the output to the Vegeta report tool to generate a report of the test results.

Analyze the Results

The report generated by Vegeta provides detailed information about the test results, including the response time, the number of requests and successes, and any errors that occurred. We can use this information to identify any performance or scalability issues in our application and take steps to address them.

Scalability Testing

Overview

Scalability testing is a crucial part of performance testing that evaluates the ability of a system to handle increasing workloads, whether it's the number of users or the amount of data. Scalability testing is important to ensure that the system can handle increased traffic and perform efficiently under high load conditions.

In software development, scalability testing helps to identify the limitations of an application or system, including its hardware and software components, and determine the maximum capacity it can handle. This type of testing is important for any application that may experience sudden spikes in traffic, such as e-commerce sites during holiday shopping periods, social media sites during peak usage hours, or mobile applications during major events.

Techniques of Scalability Testing

Scalability testing can be performed in two ways: vertical scaling and horizontal scaling. Vertical scaling involves adding more resources to an existing server, such as increasing the amount of memory or processing power. This method is limited by the maximum capacity of the server, and once that limit is reached, the only option is to upgrade the hardware. Horizontal scaling, on the other hand, involves adding more servers to handle the increased workload. This approach is more scalable than vertical scaling and allows for better resource utilization.

To perform scalability testing, it is important to define the goals of the test, including the number of concurrent users or requests, the duration of the test, and the expected response times. Once the goals are defined, it is necessary to create a test plan that includes scenarios that simulate the expected load on the system.

Once the test plan is created, the next step is to execute the test using the chosen tool. The tool will generate reports that show the response times, error rates, and throughput of the system. Based on the results of the test, it is possible to identify performance bottlenecks and areas for optimization.

There are several tools available for scalability testing in Go language, including Apache JMeter, Fortio, Boom, K6, and Goad. By performing scalability testing, it is possible to identify performance bottlenecks and optimize the system for better performance and scalability.

Exploring Apache JMeter

Apache JMeter is a popular open-source performance testing tool that can be used for load testing, stress testing, and scalability testing. It allows you to simulate different scenarios and test the performance of your web application or service. JMeter is written in Java and can be used with any language that supports HTTP.

Using Apache JMeter with Go

To use Apache JMeter with Go, you can follow the steps below:

Download and install Java

Apache JMeter requires Java to be installed on your system. You can download the latest version of Java from the official website.

Download and extract Apache JMeter

You can download the latest version of Apache JMeter from the official website. Once downloaded, extract the contents of the archive to a folder on your system.

Install the JMeter plugins manager

The JMeter plugins manager is a community-driven project that provides additional plugins and functionality to JMeter. You can install it by following the instructions on the official website.

Start JMeter

To start JMeter, navigate to the folder where you extracted the contents of the archive and run the jmeter.bat (Windows) or jmeter.sh (Linux) script.

Create a test plan

A test plan is a JMeter project that defines the scenario you want to test. You can create a test plan by following the steps outlined in the JMeter user manual.

Configure JMeter to work with Go

To configure JMeter to work with Go, you need to add a HTTP Request sampler to your test plan and configure it to send requests to your Go application. You can also configure JMeter to use multiple threads and/or multiple machines to simulate a large number of users.

Run the test

Once you have configured your test plan, you can run the test by clicking the Run button in JMeter. JMeter will then simulate the scenario you defined and generate a report with the results.

Procedure to Run Apache JMeter Testing

Below is a sample JMeter test plan for performing scalability testing on a Go application:

Add a Thread Group

Right-click on the Test Plan and select Add -> Threads (Users) -> Thread Group.

Configure the Thread Group

In the Thread Group panel, set the Number of Threads (users) to the number of concurrent users you want to simulate. You can also set the Ramp-Up Period to gradually increase the number of users over time.

Add a HTTP Request sampler

Right-click on the Thread Group and select Add -> Sampler -> HTTP Request.

Configure the HTTP Request sampler

In the HTTP Request panel, set the Server Name or IP to the hostname or IP address of your Go application. Set the Port Number to the port your Go application is running on. Set the Path to the URL of the endpoint you want to test.

Add a Response Assertion

Right-click on the HTTP Request sampler and select Add -> Assertions -> Response Assertion.

Configure the Response Assertion

In the Response Assertion panel, set the Test Field to Response Code. Set the Pattern to the HTTP response code you expect to receive (e.g. 200).

Run the test

Click the Run button in JMeter to start the test. JMeter will simulate the scenario you defined and generate a report with the results.

Overall, Apache JMeter is a powerful tool for performing scalability testing on Go applications. By following the steps outlined above, you can easily set up JMeter to simulate a large number of users and test the performance of your application.

Sample Program to Run Scalability Testing with Apache JMeter

Below is an example of how you could create a scalability test scenario using Apache JMeter:

Install Apache JMeter and open it.

Create a new Test Plan by selecting File > New.

Add a Thread Group to the Test Plan by right-clicking on the Test Plan and selecting Add > Threads (Users) > Thread Group.

In the Thread Group settings, set the number of threads (i.e., users) to simulate and the ramp-up period (i.e., the time period over which the threads will be started).

Add one or more Samplers to the Thread Group by right-clicking on the Thread Group and selecting Add > Sampler.

Configure the Samplers to simulate different types of requests to the system, such as HTTP requests.

Add one or more Listeners to the Test Plan by right-clicking on the Test Plan and selecting Add > Listener.

Configure the Listeners to capture and display the test results, such as response times and error rates.

Save the Test Plan and run it.

Monitor the system's performance during the test and analyze the results to identify any bottlenecks or issues.

By following these steps, you can create a scalability test scenario using Apache JMeter to test the performance and scalability of your system. You can then use the results of the test to identify any issues and make improvements to your system to ensure that it can handle increasing amounts of load and traffic.

Summary

In this chapter, we discussed various types of performance testing, such as load testing, stress testing, and scalability testing. We also looked at the importance of performance testing and how it helps organizations to identify performance issues before they affect users.

We also discussed the Vegeta tool, which is an open-source HTTP load testing tool that can be used to generate a large number of requests to a server and analyze its response. Vegeta is written in Go language, which makes it fast and efficient.

We went on to discuss how to perform load testing, stress testing, and scalability testing using Vegeta. In load testing, we simulated a large number of users accessing a website simultaneously to identify how the website performs under a heavy load. We used Vegeta to simulate a large number of requests and analyze the website's response time and throughput.

In stress testing, we tried to determine the website's maximum capacity by simulating a higher load than what the website can handle. This was done by increasing the number of requests per second until the website could no longer handle the load. We used Vegeta to gradually increase the load and determine the website's maximum capacity.

In scalability testing, we tested the website's ability to handle an increasing number of users or requests by gradually increasing the load and monitoring the website's performance. We used Apache JMeter to simulate a large number of users and requests and analyzed how the website's performance changed as the load increased.

Overall, performance testing is an essential aspect of software development, and tools like Vegeta can help organizations to identify and fix performance issues before they affect users. Load testing, stress testing, and scalability testing are some of the techniques used to perform performance testing, and Vegeta and JMeter can be used to perform these tests efficiently. By understanding and implementing these testing techniques, organizations can ensure that their software performs optimally under different conditions and user loads.

Thank You

Epilogue

As we reach the end of "Mastering Go Network Automation," it is crucial to reflect on the wealth of knowledge and skills that you, the reader, have acquired throughout this journey. Network automation has become an essential aspect of modern network management, allowing administrators to enhance efficiency, scalability, and security within their environments. In this book, we have covered a wide range of topics to provide a comprehensive understanding of network automation and the tools required to implement it successfully.

In the beginning, we explored the foundations of network automation with the EVE-NG network simulator and the Go programming language. You learned how to set up your own network automation lab, giving you a controlled environment to experiment with and practice your new skills. This foundation set the stage for a deeper exploration of network automation concepts and techniques.

We then delved into the world of service mesh and its role in automation. By understanding how service mesh can simplify network operations, you gained valuable insights into deploying ingress controllers and implementing service mesh with Linkerd. These critical topics provided you with the necessary background to navigate the complexities of modern network management.

As we progressed, the importance of containerization became evident, and we discussed container-native storage and container storage management with Docker. Additionally, we covered automating SSL certificates, firewall configuration, and network policies, all essential aspects of maintaining a secure network.

The book also addressed monitoring and performance tuning, teaching you how to keep a watchful eye on container performance and roll out updates automatically. By understanding the importance of monitoring, you can now ensure the stability and resilience of your network infrastructure.

Lastly, we explored performance testing strategies such as load testing, stress testing, and scalability testing. By learning how to identify performance bottlenecks and optimize your network, you can now utilize tools like Vegeta and Apache JMeter to improve your network's performance and reliability.

As you look back on the material covered in "Mastering Go Network Automation," take a moment to appreciate the progress you have made. Armed with this knowledge, you are now better equipped to face the challenges of network administration and automation in an ever-changing technological landscape.

However, it is essential to remember that the learning journey does not end here. As a network administrator, it is vital to stay informed of emerging technologies, best practices, and evolving tools to ensure your network remains secure and efficient. Keep exploring, experimenting, and refining your skills, and don't be afraid to seek out additional resources to expand your understanding further.

Thank you for choosing "Mastering Go Network Automation" as your guide on this journey. We hope that the knowledge you've gained will serve you well as you continue to develop your skills and shape the future of network automation. As you face new challenges and embrace new opportunities, remember that the best way to master a subject is through continuous learning and adaptation. Keep pushing the boundaries, and always strive for excellence in your work as a network administrator.

Made in United States
Orlando, FL
28 April 2023

32574373R00115